From Fear to Serenity
with
Anthony de Mello

From Fear to Serenity with Anthony de Mello

Thomas G. Casey, SJ, and
Margaret Brennan Hassett

HiddenSpring

Cover design by Joy Taylor
Book design by Lynn Else

Library of Congress Cataloging-in-Publication Data

Casey, Thomas G.
    From fear to serenity with Anthony de Mello / Thomas G. Casey and Margaret Brennan Hassett.
        p. cm.
    Includes bibliographical references (p.   ).
    ISBN 978-1-58768-066-3 (alk. paper)
    1. Spiritual life—Catholic Church. 2. De Mello, Anthony, 1931–1987. I. Hassett, Margaret Brennan. II. Title.
    BX2350.3.C375 2011
    248.4'82—dc22
                                                                    2010050867

Published by
HiddenSpring
an imprint of Paulist Press
997 Macarthur Boulevard
Mahwah, New Jersey 07430

www.paulistpress.com

Printed and bound in the
United States of America

Peggy dedicates this book with much love to
Jack, Mairead, Jack, Will, Teddy, Graham, Ben, Justine,
Lily, Greta, and Henry

and Tom, with much love to
Rachel, Rebecca, Sarah, and Joshua

The Master would frequently assert that holiness was less a matter of what one did than of what one *allowed* to happen.

—Anthony de Mello

Contents

The Song of Anthony de Mello

by Rev. James Martin, SJ

Anthony de Mello, SJ (1931–1987), was an Indian Jesuit priest and one of the great spiritual masters of our time. Although de Mello was known primarily within the Catholic community for his writings and conferences, his influence transcended religious boundaries; by the end of his life, de Mello's unique spirituality was enabling people from almost every faith to approach God more easily. Among those people I happily include myself.

As a young Jesuit novice more than twenty years ago, I first encountered de Mello's genius in his book *The Song of the Bird*, a delightful compendium of parable-like tales that artfully combine Christian morality and Eastern characters along with de Mello's trademark wisdom. They captivated me immediately. From there I moved on to perhaps his most popular book, *Sadhana: A Way to God*, and was forever hooked. There is something irresistibly inviting about his approach—at once grounded in Christianity but free enough to embrace the time-tested wisdom of other spiritual traditions.

De Mello was deeply influenced, and guided, by the spirit of St. Ignatius Loyola, the founder of the Society of Jesus (the Jesuits), the religious order to which Tony belonged. Not only did he possess a profound understanding of Ignatius's Spiritual Exercises—a four-week program for prayer, focusing on the life of Christ—he was also an experienced spiritual director able to help people, in a practical way, "find God in all things," as the Ignatian dictum has it. (For those who are interested, de Mello's admirers have collected an invaluable book of his notes on the Exercises, entitled *Seek God Everywhere*.)

De Mello's encounter with Ignatian spirituality influenced his work in another way as well. One of the hallmarks of the Ignatian way of prayer is the free use of one's imagination. St. Ignatius asks us, in the Spiritual Exercises, to imaginatively place ourselves in scenes from the Gospel. So one reads a Gospel passage and does not merely think about it; one imagines oneself *within* it and asks: What do I see? What do I hear? What do I smell? What do I taste? What do I feel? As one writer has said, one doesn't merely look at Jesus' baptism; one stands knee-deep in the Jordan River with him.

De Mello's provocative reflections, parables, stories, tales, and aphorisms ask us to do the same thing: creatively use our imagination and think of life and of God in brand-new ways. For God to work within us in new ways, we first need to be open enough to think in new ways. As Jesus himself first did with his parables, de Mello invites us to see God in unexpected places and in unexpected people and at unexpected times.

De Mello's work was not without controversy. At one point after his death, the Vatican issued a warning that "certain passages" might be harmful to readers. (Some of the discomfort *may* have stemmed from the fact that de Mello felt free to use Eastern spiritual practices in his recommendations for prayer techniques.) I'm no theologian or academic, but I can say that, in my own reading of de Mello, I've only encountered a freeing spirit that encourages me to think of God as always greater than what I have previously imagined—more compassionate, more loving, more free, more surprising, more generous. De Mello's spirituality has helped me draw closer to Christ, and to God the Father—and of course to the Spirit.

This new book by Thomas G. Casey, SJ, and Margaret Brennan Hassett brings together a wealth of de Mello's wisdom, and provides an excellent introduction to the man who taught so many that God is, as St. Augustine wrote, "nearer to me than I am to myself." Read it, and find the freedom to meet God in a new, and perhaps surprising, way.

James Martin, SJ, is a Jesuit priest, the culture editor of *America* magazine, and the author of several books, including *The Jesuit Guide to (Almost) Everything, My Life with the Saints,* and *Becoming Who You Are: Insights on the True Self from Thomas Merton and Other Saints.*

Acknowledgments

We would like to acknowledge our debt to the late, great Indian Jesuit priest and spiritual master Anthony de Mello (1931–1987), who taught us so many creative ways to pray. What we have learned, we have passed on to you. Father James Martin was kind enough to contribute a gracious and elegant foreword to this book—thank you!

A special thank-you goes to Jack Kehoe for his constant support and unflagging enthusiasm, and for generously going beyond the call of duty in so many ways. Our gratitude goes to Kevin Carrizo di Camillo of HiddenSpring/Paulist Press for editing the script in such a careful and painstaking manner. We thank Michael and Mary Casey for helpful feedback on an early draft, and Paul Casey for his creative input.

It was Father Lawrence Boadt, CSP, the former president, publisher, and editorial director of Paulist Press, who initially accepted our project. Despite his serious (and ultimately terminal) cancer, he continued to work with us. May he rest in peace.

A New Way of Living

Going Beyond Fear

Tony de Mello used to tell the story of a spiritual seeker who had arrived at a deep and loving union with God. His disciples were intensely curious about what the experience was like, but the master was most reluctant to say anything about the matter. One day his own son tried to pry the secret from him, and in a rare moment of candor, the father shared his feelings. "I felt like a fool," he said. "Why?" asked the son. "Because," the father replied, "it was like going to enormous trouble to enter a house by climbing a ladder and breaking the window, only to realize afterwards that the front door had been open the whole time" (*One Minute Wisdom*, 177).

Although the journey into ourselves and to God can often take a long time, in many ways it is a journey without distance, because we travel from where we are now to where we have, in fact, always been. We have been standing in front of something wonderful all our lives but have never noticed it.

We can always discover reasons to be afraid. We find ourselves in situations that are simply beyond us, where we feel we cannot cope, we cannot pull through. We get hurt and bruised by painful relationships, and we fear that someone will take advantage of us again. Even in the normal course of events, we worry about what our neighbor thinks of us and what tomorrow holds. Fear turns us in on ourselves, making us fidgety and anxious. We wonder if anyone really cares. Too much of life can be devoured by our anxieties and lack of ease. The challenge is to find a way through the maze of personal *dis-ease* to a meadow of peace. Ultimately, we do have a choice: we have the power to choose a different path. Although we can feel imprisoned by fear, it is actually something we often choose. But fear is not the only option.

There is another option—*awareness*—that opens us to the world outside, relaxing and calming us. Tony de Mello liked to tell the story of the disciple who went to a great spiritual master, eager to hear his words of wisdom. "Can you give me a pearl of wisdom to guide my life?" It happened that the master was passing that particular day in silence, so he picked up a stone tablet and wrote upon it the word *awareness*. The disciple was disappointed. After this long journey, all he got was a single word. "Can you tease out this idea?" he asked. The master took up the tablet again, and this time wrote *awareness, awareness, awareness*. The disciple was puzzled. "But what does *awareness* mean?" he asked. Once more the master took up the tablet, and when he handed it back to the disciple, the latter read the words *Awareness, awareness, awareness means—awareness* (*One Minute Wisdom*, 10).

What is awareness? It is the heart of true spirituality. In de Mello's words: "Spirituality means waking up. Most people, even though they don't know it, are asleep. They're born asleep, they live asleep, they marry in their sleep, they breed children in their sleep, they die in their sleep without ever waking up" (*Awareness*, 5).

Awareness is about coming home, about rediscovering ourselves. It is not about changing our behavior, but liberating our vision. In this book, we journey with you toward a transformative vision, in order to learn to let go instead of taking on yet another task or theory. We already have all we need right in front of us: we just cannot see it. In an ideal world, we would like to be free of all our neuroses, but even without entering a neurosis-free zone, we can be happy now, just as we are. Yogi Berra said, "You can observe a lot by just watching." De Mello invites us to look and to see for the first time. As we travel the path from fear to serenity, we will learn to look at ourselves with compassion and without judgment.

At the beginning of his book *The Power of Now*, Eckhart Tolle tells the story of a beggar who has been sitting in the same spot for more than thirty years. One day a stranger passes by. The stranger has no money to give, but he asks the beggar about the box upon which he is sitting. The beggar says it is nothing special, just an old box. The stranger tells him to look inside it. The beggar feels this is pointless; he has been sitting on this box forever, and he is convinced it holds nothing, and certainly so surprises. But the stranger persists. Finally, the beggar opens the box and is amazed to discover that it is full of gold (*The Power of Now: A Guide to Spiritual Enlightenment*, Novato, CA: New World Library, 2004, 11).

What you hold in your hands is not merely a book; it is a path to hope, a guide to prayer, and a call to see in a new way. It is an invitation to go beyond the ego and to drop any addiction to worry. It is a call to breathe easily and become aware. So please do not limit yourself only to reading it. Try out the prayer exercises. Stop to reflect on the stories you read. Underline phrases. Make notes in the margins. If something you read touches you in a special way, share it with a friend. Above all, let what touches you inform your life choices, so that you outgrow old ways of thinking and usher in a world of new promises and possibilities. Do not rush to get to the end of the book. Relax and take time to enjoy the journey. Read what follows in an unhurried manner. Pause regularly to consider what you are reading, instead of feeling you have to rush forward to the next page or chapter. After you read a chapter, try out the exercises it provides on awareness and prayer. The key is not to acquire a lot of information, but to let a few profound truths sink into your heart. Give yourself time to absorb them. That way you will gain great spiritual profit from this journey.

You do not need to be hooked on fear. You can tune into a more liberating wavelength. As we travel in the spirit of Tony de Mello, we highlight the importance of self-knowledge, meditation, and living in the present moment; we emphasize the power of vision and creativity; and we underline the link between breathing and relaxation, between body and spirit. This positive book emphasizes a new way of seeing. You need not be isolated in your own anxieties or inner turmoil. You do have a choice. Do not give fear the permission to block you from living. Cultivating your inner life will help you find freedom. It will bring you into harmony with your Eternal Source. It will put you in touch with a world that is visited by God and that is happily "upset" by God's law of love. Ultimately, you can live for something larger and more adventurous than self-obsession; you can become connected with the biggest force in the universe—God.

STRUCTURE

Each chapter of this book has stories, key phrases, and practical exercises.

Stories. The stories in each chapter are aimed at your heart. Let them stay with you, not only while you are reading the book, but also when you put it down—when you are driving or doing household chores. Retell these stories to yourself during the course of the day so that their transforming power can sink in.

Key phrases. In each chapter there is at least one key phrase, which is *italicized*. The key phrase expresses a core principle in a shorthand, easy-to-remember way. These phrases are not intellectual puzzles, mind riddles, or Zen koans. They are addressed to your heart. When it comes to prayer, you often have to leave your mind to come to your senses. Saint Augustine (354–430 AD), the towering intellectual of the early centuries of Christianity, was once trying to figure out the mystery of the Trinity while he walked along a beach. He came across a boy who was running to the sea and then back again with a bucket of water. Each time he got back to the beach with his bucketful of water, the boy poured it into a small hole in the sand. "What are you doing?" Augustine asked. "I'm trying to put the ocean into this hole," replied the boy. "But that's impossible," retorted Augustine. "Just as impossible as trying to fit the infinity of God into your little mind," replied the boy before vanishing from his sight.

There is a marvelous passage in Saint Augustine's book *Confessions*: Just before his conversion, Augustine was in a garden. He broke down sobbing under a fig tree. At that moment he heard what sounded like a child's voice saying, "*Tolle, lege*"—"Take and read." He picked up a book with the Letters of Saint Paul and read a passage that gave him peace and serenity. Then and there he resolved to give his life to God (Augustine, *Confessions*, book 8, chapter 12).

Practical exercises. Tony de Mello offers a daily routine of simple physical exercises that help release the fear that so easily courses through your body. But these physical exercises also relax your inner being, just like the spiritual exercises he proposes. In the spirit of de Mello, here you will find various practical exercises, from breathing to awareness to meditation. These exercises have changed the lives of countless people. They could transform your life, too. As well as getting you in touch with your own heart, these exercises will give you a taste for God's love that will have you hungry for more. Try them out. Put them into practice. Dare to believe in their power.

INVITATION

You already have the power to let God transform your life. You can exercise that power by applying this book to your life as you read it. All you need is a tiny bit of willingness to open your heart and let God in. The stories and exercises will help you attain greater peace and enable you to live for something larger, through revealing the riches that lie hidden within your heart and through bringing to light God's immense love for you. Now that you have taken up this book and are reading it, we pray that it will carry you from worry to trust, from unease to serenity, from the parched desert to the clear flowing waters. Most of all, we pray that it will deepen your friendship with God, guiding you into a space that nourishes your deepest hungers and nurtures your greatest longings.

CHAPTER ONE

Why Tony de Mello?

Tony de Mello was an Indian Jesuit who blended the best of East and West into spiritual teachings that have touched millions of people around the world. His way promised a release from worry and anxiety through seeing life in a new way. He died suddenly in 1987, but his appeal is timeless and his message still resonates across the world. He communicates deep truths about the human spirit, and the most profound truths always endure.

Tony de Mello had a magnetic presence. He was dazzling, electrifying his audiences with his insight and wit, with his unique blend of deep spirituality and human groundedness. He was captivating, even if you did not always agree with him; the truth is that he often disagreed with himself. He changed positions several times during his lifetime. Like many great mystics, he was given to paradox, uttering flagrantly contradictory statements. He also delighted in prodding and provoking his hearers.

Tony de Mello left us millions of words: in his books, videos, and tapes, and in the many books written about him. Yet despite all these words, there is something surprisingly elusive about the man himself. Who was he? What made him tick?

Was de Mello the pious Jesuit novice who lived by the rules and volunteered for the most humiliating jobs? Or was he the free spirit of the last years of his life, intent on setting rules and regulations aside, seeking total "freedom"? Was he the demanding coun-

selor who could explode in anger at certain clients during group
therapy sessions, or the entertainer who confessed he wanted to die
telling a joke? Was he the master wordsmith who could tell stories
for hours, or the mystic who wanted to leave words completely
behind? The young priest who fasted, prayed, and lived in poverty, or
the mature retreat giver who jetted around the world to give semi-
nars? Were some of his teachings incompatible with the doctrine of
the Catholic Church, as the notification of the Vatican's Congregation for the Doctrine of the Faith stated, or did he seek to remain
faithful to the Church? There is truth in every one of these claims,
because in many ways Tony was a mass of contradictions.

Despite his contradictory nature, Tony steadily made his way
toward serenity, though he never fully left fear behind. In his psyche,
he underwent moments of what the Jesuit poet Gerard Manley
Hopkins once described, in his short and anguished poem "No
Worst, There is None," as "cliffs of fall / frightful, sheer, no-man-
fathomed." In a letter to a friend a year before he died, Tony
described how he felt in the grip of crushing despair, deep fear, and
loneliness. Like all of us, Tony had his dark moments. He once said
that enlightenment does not magically change a person's tempera-
ment: an impractical person does not suddenly become down-to-
earth; an incessant talker does not become mystically silent. People
stay largely as they are, but what does change is the way they *see*
things. They view the world and themselves with eyes full of wonder; they see everything in a freer and more detached way. Fear is part
of the human condition and is never permanently uprooted or erad-
icated. Yet we can choose not to let it dictate the agenda of our lives.

Tony did not enter a state of enlightenment devoid of fear, for
anyone who tries out new things and takes risks will still experience
fearful moments. But what he did learn was not to live out of fear.
He succeeded in being himself, in joyfully singing his song. Saint
Irenaeus says that *the glory of God is the fully alive human being* (Irenaeus,

Against the Heresies, book 4, chapter 20). Tony was that kind of human being, fully alive and so human. He could hold any audience willingly captive for hours, by turns delighting, shocking, and moving his listeners almost to tears. If he were an actor, his performances would have earned him an Oscar. He would walk into a room, with a beaming smile and a twinkle in his eyes, sit down on a large high table, his back ramrod straight, and his legs playfully dangling in the air below. Without a single note or cue, he would simply start talking. He talked about everything: how to pray, how to accept yourself, how to drop attachments—the importance of messing up in life (yes!)—the mystical wisdom of Saint Teresa of Avila, Meister Eckhart, and the Bhagavad Gita—and why we should kill the Buddha if we meet him on the road. He was like a DJ who plays a song by U2, then a jazz standard by Ella Fitzgerald, and sandwiches a Mozart aria between them. All the time he told story after story after story. He claimed that a story was the shortest way between the heart of the human being and truth.

Tony de Mello was eclectic, borrowing liberally from all traditions and none at all: Christianity, Hinduism, Buddhism, Hassidic Judaism, Sufism, Taoism, psychology—you name it, he used it. His spirituality straddled East and West. Although he made use of insights from everywhere, he definitely considered himself a Christian (he was, after all, a Jesuit priest), although he had a pet hate for phony religion of any kind. He told the story of a known sinner who was excommunicated and banned from entering the church. In desperation the man turned to God. "Lord, they won't allow me in because I'm a sinner." "What are you moaning about?" God replied. "They won't let me in either!" (*The Prayer of the Frog,* 105).

Tony realized there was good in many different religions and traditions, and he used whatever gems of wisdom he could find in order to help people discover the unexplored richness of their own faith. Does this mean he had nothing original to say? Not at all!

What was original about Tony was the marvelous way he combined these different streams into a flowing river, and in a manner that looked effortless, even though you sensed it was the fruit of many years of effort, of countless hours of prayer, and of mystical experience. He used stories to overcome the obstacles between his listeners and him. If someone argues with us, we easily get into counterarguments, but a story is incontrovertible: you can't argue with it. It gets under the radar screen of reason and touches the heart.

Anthony de Mello was born in Bombay (Mumbai), India, on September 4, 1931. His parents had grown up on the southwest coast of India, in Goa, a former Portuguese colony. Goa has a long Jesuit connection. It was evangelized by the famous Jesuit missionary Saint Francis Xavier four hundred years earlier. Tony was educated by the Jesuits in Bombay. He excelled at anything he turned his hands to, and was incredibly popular with his classmates. He entered the Jesuits at sixteen years of age, as soon as he finished school. Oozing with self-righteousness, he had a holier-than-thou kind of piety as a teenager. He was a bit of an overzealous novice, too much of a "Holy Joe," with no time for those who deviated in the least way from Roman Catholic teaching. But although he had a large dose of spirituality, he had terribly little self-knowledge.

Tony was sent to Barcelona in 1952 to study philosophy for three years. He began to read the giants of Spanish mysticism in the original language—Teresa of Avila, John of the Cross, and, of course, the founder of the Jesuits, Ignatius of Loyola. He returned to India in 1955 and taught in a Jesuit high school in Bombay for three years, enlivening students with his wit and stories, and gradually introducing them to the world of spirituality. In 1958, he began four years of theological studies in Pune, India. In these years before Vatican II, theology was still taught in Latin. But there was a rising consciousness among certain professors and students about the importance of integrating Catholicism into Indian culture. For his part, Tony used his spare time to read the holy texts of Hinduism and to visit Hindu ashrams. In March of 1961, he was ordained a priest.

His superiors decided that he should become a spiritual guide, and to that end they sent him first to the United States to study counseling at Loyola University in Chicago, and then later to Rome to study spirituality at the Pontifical Gregorian University. Tony spent a year at Loyola, Chicago, starting in 1963. He was to learn a lot from his experience there. For the first time in his life, he was studying with laypeople, many of whom had put a certain distance between themselves and traditional religious practice. They were not satisfied with conventional or pat answers, and he felt challenged to articulate his beliefs in a way that spoke to the probing questions of these educated laypeople. He also met students who asked him about Indian mysticism, and this spurred him to explore the non-Christian religions of India more deeply, not just by reading about them, but in concrete ways; for example, by himself engaging in Buddhist meditation. In addition, he discovered how important psychology was in the world of spirituality. Grace builds on nature, it does not replace nature. Therefore, it is important that one's human nature is sound, so that grace can build on this foundation, and elevate nature even higher. It steadily dawned upon Tony that a lot of so-called spiritual problems were, in fact, psychological problems.

When he was sent to the Gregorian University, Tony did not take to the way his professors taught spirituality. To him, their approach seemed dry and formal, a barren way of communicating something so life-giving and transformative. He only stayed a year in Rome and returned to India in 1965, where he began working in a poor village, sharing the simple life of the local people. But after a few years of this work, his superiors, recognizing his great charisma and many gifts, put him in charge of a large community of young Jesuits in formation. He surprised everyone by refusing to occupy the large and relatively luxurious quarters assigned to him, and instead choosing to live in one of the smallest and simplest rooms in the entire house. He drew on his studies in spirituality and psychology to form these young Jesuits in a way that combined deep prayer and solid self-knowledge.

In 1972, building on his experience with these young Jesuits, Tony set up an institute at Pune for more mature Jesuits, with concrete experience of ministry, to help them take time out to learn how to integrate psychology and spirituality into their lives and ministries. He called this initiative *sadhana*, a Sanskrit word that denotes a means, way, practice, or discipline leading to a spiritual goal.

In 1974, he was elected to represent his brother Jesuits from the Bombay area at a world congregation of Jesuits in Rome. While there, he was invited to guide the group in prayer. Instead of taking them to a quiet chapel, he brought them to the noisiest room in the whole house, with Roman traffic blaring outside. To everyone's surprise, he managed to lead the group into deep prayer in this most challenging of settings. He was illustrating the point that God is not locked up in a sanctuary, but can be found everywhere. He was somewhat like the character Stephen Dedalus in James Joyce's *Ulysses*, who points to a noisy street and says, "That is God." This incident gave Tony exposure and an international platform—invitations began to pour in from all over the world. In 1978, he relocated his counseling and spiritual institute in the town of Lonavla, a short distance from Pune, and gave it the name Sadhana Institute.

In this last decade of his life, Tony became somewhat of a spiritual celebrity. Some would say he became intoxicated with his own aura. He became accustomed to being in the spotlight. Some individuals felt that just being near him would set them "free." They hung on every word of this spiritual titan. It was not easy to handle that kind of power. But overall, Tony did not get derailed by his guru-like status. For the most part, he stayed centered. Although he liked being the life and soul of the party, he knew it was not about him. He was more interested in ordinary people than in any cult around himself. He wanted to bolster their faith.

Above all, Tony wanted to jolt "religious" people out of a false sense of piety. So he was deliberately provocative, and he regularly exaggerated for effect, a bit like the Hebrew prophets. You cannot take everything he said—or wrote—at face value. You have to subtract some of the hyperbole, you have to read between the lines, to get the underlying thrust of what he was saying. Tony delighted in upsetting the applecart, and if you read his writings, you may wrongly believe that he was out to destroy things, to attack every sacred cow in sight. In fact, his real interest was to get people in touch with the spiritual life and to help them find God.

For instance, you can get the impression reading Tony's books that he had little time for Jesus. It is certainly true that he did not say much about Jesus. But this may be due to the principal audience he addressed during his lifetime, an audience primarily made up of priests, nuns, and religiously committed laypeople. They thought they knew a lot about Jesus and Christianity, but in reality they were often ignorant of basic things; for instance, they had little *felt* sense of the reality of God's love for them as unique and irreplaceable individuals. Although they never stopped talking about Jesus in their teaching and preaching, many of them had not really taken in what following Jesus meant for their lives. They were "professional" religious—and came up with ingenious ways to avoid the challenge of truly following the path of Christ. Tony was trying to give them a wake-up call, to wake up these people to being human, to help them recognize their own blindness and self-deception. If he could succeed in doing that, he felt that the message of Christ would get across much better.

Tony's appeal is not just his undeniable charisma, because charisma alone is not enough to make anyone a great mystical teacher. The world is full of charismatic figures who have used this gift for their own ends and to the detriment of others. There was more than just personal magnetism to Tony de Mello. When the scales are balanced, the end result of his life's work is highly positive. He led great numbers of people to a true spirituality along a simple yet profound path. He guided them from pure self-absorption to a search for something more profound in their lives. Anyone genuinely seeking to find a spiritual path will benefit enormously from Tony de Mello's wisdom. At the same time he is not everyone's proverbial cup of tea. Many people are more comfortable with the clearly demarcated parameters of religion: go to Mass, say your prayers, and make your donations. But for those who want something deeper from their religion, and for those who want to go beyond the emptiness they often feel in secularized society, Tony offers a new and nourishing language of faith.

Tony told the story of a gifted inventor who came upon an ancient tribe in a faraway country (*The Prayer of the Frog*, 7–8). The tribe needed fire to keep warm and to cook. But the members of the tribe were unable to make fire by themselves. They were forced to pay for the services of a man from a neighboring village, who would arrive and rub two stones together until a spark was ignited. It was laborious and time-consuming. Luckily, the inventor had developed a much more efficient and straightforward way of making fire. He happily and generously taught this method to the people of the tribe, who hailed him as a quasi-messiah. Everyone was profoundly grateful, except for one small group within the tribe. The problem was that this small group was particularly powerful. It was made up of the priests. They were dismayed that the inventor had become so popular, and feared that their own power and influence were on the wane. So they came up with a chilling plan: they decided to murder the inventor. Knowing how much he was loved by the people, they made his death seem like an accident. Moreover, afterward they built a huge shrine to his memory. At the center of the shrine was a life-size picture of the inventor and a number of small fires to honor his life and achievements. Every day people of the tribe arrived to give thanks to God for the inventor and what he had given the village. But as the years passed by, people forgot the secret of making fire, and all that remained was a decrepit old shrine with some burned-out embers in front of it.

We can all benefit from asking ourselves: "Where is the fire now?" The spirituality that makes us truly alive is a living fire, but there is always the danger of extinguishing the fire for safety reasons, and surviving with some ineffective substitute instead. Organized religion can easily keep us in a box and degenerate into a counterfeit spirituality. True spirituality is liberating.

The fire of love can set your whole life alight. Strangely, self-proclaimed "religious" people are sometimes the very ones who quench this fire, because religion can easily be used to control, whereas spirituality is about surrender. Too many ministers and priests guard the approach to the holy of holies as though they owned it. Too many harden into starched-shirt administrators. They no longer feel the breath of the Spirit that once inspired them, and all that remains is only a religion that is too full of self and too empty of God.

How many people leave church after Sunday Mass or service believing the astonishing truth that they are God's gift to the world? And not because they have theology degrees, but because of the fire of their love? Unfortunately, too many people are limited by the rules of religion. Too many people are stuck in their heads. You cannot reach your heart while you are in your head, and you won't find fire in your head. Spirituality sets you free, it is liberating. Spirituality sets you on fire. "Someday, after mastering the winds, the waves, the tides and gravity, we shall harness for God the energies of love, and then, for a second time in the history of the world, the human being will have discovered fire" (Teilhard de Chardin, *The Phenomenon of Man*).

We hope you find truth here in the best sense of the word, the kind of truth that gives you serenity. We hope you attain serenity with the help of the relatively simple steps we outline here. It would be wonderful if this book could help you find something more valuable and significant in your life.

REVIEW

Story. Please reflect upon the story about finding fire. Take time out to mull over this story and relate it to your life. Let it sink into your heart. It can take a while to absorb the message of a story. We can dutifully nod our heads to it, but allowing it to enter our hearts is another matter. There is a big difference between head-knowledge and heart-knowledge. The distance between the head and the heart is literally only fifteen inches, but it can take a lifetime to make the journey between the two. When we let a story sink in, we get in touch with our hearts. The emotional connection a story makes is capable of overcoming our resistance to change, giving us the freedom to begin our journey toward serenity.

Key phrase. *The glory of God is the fully alive human being.* You are created to be fully alive! To be fully alive means arriving at your full potential. Everyone has a song to sing, and it would be a tragedy if you never sang your special song. To actualize your full potential means using all your physical, emotional, intellectual, and spiritual resources. The following questions will help you decide to what extent you are realizing your potential at the physical, emotional, intellectual, and spiritual levels of life:

- At the *physical* level, do you take care of your body? Do you have a healthy diet? Do you get adequate rest? Do you get physical exercise?
- At the *emotional* level, can you give proper expression to your emotions? Do you love? Do you feel loved?

- At the *intellectual* level, do you nourish your mind with inspiring thoughts and ideas?
- At the *spiritual* level, are you aware of God's presence in your life? Do you communicate with God?

To give birth to all your resources, you need to develop a positive image of yourself, others, and God. This transforming journey takes a lifetime. Remember this: No one becomes fully human and fully alive by accident. You must *want* to develop, *choose* to improve, and *strive* to grow, and you must persist in this commitment. Full life is not a state of drowsy contentment, but the happiness you feel when you are employing your powers to the full, when you are blooming and flourishing.

Becoming more alive is not just about *your* effort, however. It is, primarily, a gift of God. And yet—*you become whatever you set your heart upon*—whatever you think about, whatever you desire. Set your heart upon finding God, and you will find serenity. You will gain greater confidence in yourself. You will find new life in your relationships. You will learn to enjoy life more. You will find happiness in loving others.

The activity below is designed to get you in touch with God in your life. This is a Tony de Mello exercise (*Sadhana*, 11f), and its goal is to help you live life in the moment, to taste and savor it. When you begin to live in the here and now, you are already well on the way to becoming a mystic.

EXERCISE: EXPERIENCING GOD THROUGH YOUR BODY

Sit in a chair, adopt a comfortable posture, and keep your back straight. Close your eyes or half close them. Now, become aware of the sensations in your body. Start with your shoulders. Become aware of the sensation of your clothes touching your shoulders. Feel your upper back, and become aware of the clothes touching this part of your back. If your back is against the chair, become aware of the feel of the chair against your back. Continue through your middle and lower back. Become aware of your hands as they touch each other, your lap, or your sides. Become aware of your buttocks and thighs as they press against the chair. Feel the sensation of your socks on your feet or the touch of your feet against the floor. And when you have gone through these different parts of your body, repeat the sequence once more, starting with your shoulders and finishing with your feet.

Now reflect for a moment that you would be unable to feel any sensation at all were it not for God's support. So now try to feel God's power in and through each of the sensations of your body. Feel God touching you in the touch of the clothes on your shoulder, back, buttocks, thighs, legs, and so on.

This exercise may strike you as strange, precisely because we often expect our experience of God to be unusual and out of the ordinary. It can be hard to believe that we could experience God in such an ordinary and undramatic way. Yet the first time that God was heard in our midst, it was in the helpless cry of the baby Jesus. The first sound of God on earth was not an intelligent sentence, a dramatic piece of rhetoric, or a theological insight. The first time we heard the sound of God was in a baby's cry from a manger.

We tend to search for God in extraordinary and spectacular experiences. But in the process, we dismiss (or at least diminish) the importance of our everyday experience. In order to find God, it is enough to attain inner stillness. God is already at work, touching you in the humdrum happenings of your daily life. We invite you to experience God right now.

To find peace, it is vital to become aware of God's presence in your life. Relax into the rhythm of the Divine Presence. If you can begin to tap into this presence, you will reap undreamed-of benefits and become more truly yourself in the process.

CHAPTER TWO

Preparing for Prayer

Feelings of fright and fragility can spur us to pray with greater urgency. Insecurity is also a powerful motivator. When security vanishes, we wonder where serenity can be found. Saint Teresa of Avila, a Spanish mystic who herself lived through inner turbulence, once put it this way: "God alone is enough" (*solo Dios basta*). Only God can fill our hearts. Prayer puts us in touch with God, who is bigger than all our fears.

But how can we begin to pray? Not surprisingly, in prayer, as in much else of life, there are some simple basics that get us going; little details are hugely important. Tony de Mello's book *Sadhana: A Way to God* is recognized by many as a spiritual classic, and it is striking that, when it comes to prayer, he does not overlook the importance of small details. On the contrary, he pays careful attention to them. Place and time are really important. And so are awareness and breath. Let us look at each of these factors in turn.

SACRED SPACE

Although in principle we can pray anywhere, even on a crowded subway, when we first set out on the journey, an atmosphere of external quiet helps inner quiet to develop. Find a peaceful atmosphere or ambience. It does not have to be completely quiet; for instance, as background music, you may find meditative hymns helpful or a recording of natural sounds. Glaring overhead lights can be intrusive; subdued lighting is often preferable. Choose a place of prayer where you will not be distracted, a place where you are unlikely to be disturbed by others. It need not be large, and requires no special furnishing or equipment. At the same time, remember that beauty attracts us, and a warm and inviting space makes prayer easier. So, if it is necessary, make some simple adjustments to mark out this space as a zone of serenity. For instance, use soft fabrics, put up photographs or posters of beautiful natural scenes, place a vase of flowers here, and a bowl of fruit there. Adorn it with icons and symbols that have a calming effect. As a result, you will find that tension and stress are automatically defused once you enter this space. Once you get used to your sacred space, you will feel physically relaxed on entering it, and your thoughts will not buzz around like mosquitoes. If you can create an inviting and warm space for your prayer, it will be easier for you to pray.

However, you may decide against rearranging furniture or creating an elaborate space. You may decide simply to occupy your favorite chair or a quiet spot in the garden. You may kneel at your bed, or sit in the lotus position in a corner. You may choose to look out your living-room window at a big oak tree outside or at a stretch of blue sky, for nature can easily speak to us of God.

Tony de Mello had a novel approach to choosing a place for prayer. He often deliberately took groups to the noisiest and most distracting place he could find; for example, to a room with windows that opened onto a busy street. Amazingly, he managed to help people pray even in the midst of such a din. How did he do it? He did it by means of a technique we like to call "judo of the spirit." In Japanese, the word *judo* means "the gentle way." In judo, you use your opponent's weight and momentum against him; this means that a short and thin person can overcome a big burly opponent. De Mello placed people in a particularly noisy room and used the noise itself to their advantage. He turned the noise into a weapon against noise. He flipped the whole situation around by inviting people, not to resist the noise as a distraction, but to listen to it and to welcome it as a means of gathering and collecting their spirits.

The late Earl Woods, father of golfer Tiger Woods, used a similar method to toughen up his son. When Tiger was practicing golf as a young boy, his father would jingle coins in his pocket or stand in front of him when he was about to take a swing. He would even drop a golf bag in front of Tiger during his swing. By making a racket in the background (and more often in the foreground), Earl helped his gifted son to "zone out noise" and block out distractions. We will show you how to use noise in your favor in one of our awareness exercises later in this chapter.

SACRED TIME

Business gurus teach us that if we give all our time to urgent issues, we will never make genuine progress on what is truly important. Urgent things claim our attention immediately. But if we only turn to what is urgent, we neglect important long-term projects. Because we are prone to worry, we often panic to get the urgent things done, since they are staring us right in the face. But if we spend all our time putting out minor forest fires, we will not have time to plant new trees and help a new forest grow.

In our heart of hearts, we know prayer is vitally important. But in our everyday lives, we rarely experience prayer as urgent—unless we are in a crisis. Prayer is urgent if our house is on fire, but prayer is also vitally important if we want our house to be a home and to have a human, loving, and spiritually inviting ambience. Dwight D. Eisenhower once wisely remarked that "the urgent problems are seldom the important ones." It is all too easy to get bogged down in the urgent. It takes planning and deliberation to tackle what is important. Our daily time for prayer can easily lose out because there are so many urgent things that claim our attention, so many tasks that need to be tackled right now.

So when is the best time for prayer? The best time to pray is whenever you *can* pray. But in addition to turning to God spontaneously for a moment or two during your day, it is also vital to set up a specific formal time during the day for prayer. What time is best? There is no infallible answer. Here's a rule of thumb: the best time to pray is when you can get into prayer most easily and when you will be least likely disturbed. That may be the early morning when everything is quiet and no one else is up. It may be the late evening when everyone else has gone to bed. We ourselves prefer the early morning or, ideally, both. Listen to the following to see why.

There is a little-known side of the story of Cain and Abel from the book of Genesis (Gen 4:3–4). Abel brought a generous gift to God, the first lamb from his flock of sheep. Cain was not nearly as thoughtful. He just picked some fruit and gave it to God, but it was not the first fruit or the best; it was simply what was left over after he had had his fill. Perhaps Cain figured that by giving a gift, God would then owe him a favor that he could call on someday. But Abel was not out to get something for himself. There was nothing calculating about *his* gift. It was from a generous heart, because Abel was thinking not of himself but of God.

This is why we ourselves prefer the early morning to pray. We like to follow Abel's example and give the first fruit of our day to God by praying first thing each morning. We like to give God all our attention before we turn our attention to anyone or anything else. It is easier to focus the mind before the world starts to intrude. If we were to give God the time that remains when all our other tasks were accomplished, we would feel too much like Cain. We do not want to squeeze God between projects that claim greater time and energy. There is a saying that "a good start is half the battle." If we start off our day in tune with our deeper self and with God, it is easier to continue the day in the same vein.

As we mentioned earlier, Yogi Berra once said, "You can observe a lot just by watching." You can learn a lot by paying attention to nature. The birds that sing at dawn are already blessing the light. By turning to God at daybreak, you bless the light as well, and place your whole day within the light.

MORE BASICS

As well as place and time, there are other important items to check when you want to meditate. We suggest you take off your shoes to remind yourself that you are on holy ground. You may remember that God told Moses to take off his sandals at the burning bush because he was standing on holy ground (Exod 3:5). You are hoping to have a revelation of God, so why not present yourself barefoot before the Divine Presence? Being barefoot makes you physically more sensitive and more vulnerable. Ultimately, taking off your shoes to pray is about more than shoes; it is about taking off and stripping away whatever prevents you from experiencing this holy moment. At a physical level, it is about leaving behind the dirt and grime of the outside world that get on your shoes. At a deeper level, it is about leaving behind the dross of superficial things and the messiness of everyday life. It is also about cultivating awe and reverence. When you take off your shoes, you have to pay much more attention to where you are and where you are going, because you no longer have a protective layer around your feet. Prayer time is about paying attention to where you are and where you are going.

Loosen your clothing so that it is comfortable. It is also important to adopt a good posture. You may find a prayer stool helpful, although Westerners can find a prayer stool difficult and often find the lotus position impossible. It is better to use a reasonably comfortable seat that supports your back. Do not slouch in your chair, as this will reduce your alertness and make you sleepy. If you find it difficult to keep your back straight, use a straight-backed chair. The position you take up should be one that is both comfortable and stable. You can keep your eyes open, especially if closing your eyes leads to anxiety or sleepiness. However, for many people, keeping their eyes open is a distraction, so most find it more helpful to close their eyes.

Diet must be taken into account: do not eat immediately before praying, because it is difficult to be peaceful and serene on a full stomach. Do not smoke, drink, or eat during prayer. Turn off your cell phone. Start by lighting a candle to mark the fact that something special is about to begin.

It is also important to finish your prayer time in a peaceful and unhurried way. If you end too suddenly, you can spoil the good fruit of your meditation.

DISTRACTIONS

When you pray, you will inevitably be assailed by distractions. At the early stage of the inner journey, the mind is like a tree full of chattering monkeys jumping from one branch to another, full of curiosity and excitement. It takes time for the chattering monkeys to adjust to silence and learn to sit still. As you observe yourself meditating, you will be surprised by how frequently your thoughts wander. As you continue to meditate, the distractions may be as frequent as ever, but you will now at least be aware of them, and that is huge progress. Do not let distractions throw you off balance, no matter whether you have wonderful revelations or see smutty or violent images in your stream of consciousness. Just observe them as clouds passing over in a blue sky.

The harder you try to fight distractions, the more insistently and stubbornly they will pop up. So do not beat yourself up because of distractions. Do not let yourself get upset by them, because this will only lead to tension and disrupt your interior peace. Don't be surprised that your mind wanders: it is a sign of its vitality. Simply return gently and firmly to your meditation and prayer without letting yourself fly into a tantrum and rage. Tony de Mello wisely observed that it is impossible for the mind to be without any thoughts at all. The mind needs to think about something. So instead of trying to achieve the impossible—a state without thought—it is much more sensible to allow the mind think of something, but preferably one thing, and one thing to which it can return each time it becomes distracted.

It is not always easy to regain inner peace once you lose it. If distractions make you angry, or if you pay too much attention to them, you have lost the battle. In the event that you find it difficult to return to prayer when you are distracted, first focus on your breathing for a few minutes. Attentiveness to your breathing will bring you back to stillness, and then you can take up your prayer again. In any case, be content to let the distractions go peacefully. Drop them without any rancor or rage. But also observe the way your mind jumps from one idea or image to another. You may begin to see a pattern in these seemingly random distractions, and you may gain insight into yourself. You may also notice that you become more distracted in the evening, when your mind is processing the events of the day. You will also be more prone to distractions when you are tired.

Have you ever watched the moon at night? Clouds may often pass across its face. If your glance follows the clouds, you will lose the moon. If you keep your gaze fixed on the moon, the clouds will eventually pass. Don't fix on distractions, let them pass.

REFLECTING ON YOUR PRAYER

You can learn an enormous amount by spending a few minutes after prayer time reflecting on your experience. Ask yourself questions such as the following:

- Did I choose a helpful place for prayer?
- Was it a good time of day to pray?
- Was I energized or exhausted?
- Did I plan my prayer period beforehand?
- What touched me during prayer?
- What difficulties did I find?
- Was I able to be present to God?
- How can I use what I have learned from this prayer period to enter prayer in a deeper way the next time?

AWARENESS

Being aware is not easy. The great English novelist George Eliot puts it wonderfully in the novel *Middlemarch*: "If we had a keen vision and feeling of all ordinary human life, it would be like hearing the grass grow and the squirrel's heart beat, and we should die of that roar which lies on the other side of silence. As it is, the quickest of us walk about well wadded with stupidity" (*Middlemarch*, Forgotten Books, 2008, 145).

It is all too easy to "walk about well wadded with stupidity." It is less easy to be aware. Most of us do not notice important things. We are like the hapless policemen in Edgar Allan Poe's story "The Purloined Letter." In this story, the prefect of police in Paris, known only as Monsieur G—, is puzzled by the theft of a letter, which is now being used to blackmail the person from whom it was stolen. The prefect knows the identity of the thief, a government minister. He orders his officers to search the minister's house, but despite going through the house from top to bottom with a fine tooth comb, his men come up with nothing. The prefect of police turns for help to Dupin, a brilliant and enigmatic detective. Unlike the prefect, Dupin does not focus on the house but on the mind of the thief. He tries to figure out the minister's thought processes—and guesses correctly that the minister has not hidden the letter in an obscure place, but in the most obvious place possible.

What is hidden in the obvious fact that we breathe? A path to health and serenity. Why is this path hidden? Because we do not breathe properly. Every living person breathes. Breathing is right there in front of our noses, or actually in our noses, in our body. We breathe all the time. And yet we pay little (or no) attention to it.

Tony de Mello was fond of quoting the following saying from an Asian master: "*Your breathing is your greatest friend*. Return to it in all your troubles and you will find comfort and guidance" (*Sadhana*, 24). If this claim sounds exaggerated, it is only because most of us do not pay attention to our breathing. The truth is that practically our entire supply of oxygen and energy is thanks to our breathing. If we do not know how to breathe properly, we can become sick or can worsen existing maladies. As well as the physical benefits—including our very survival—breathing has undoubted psychic and spiritual advantages. Once we do give time and energy to our breathing, we will begin to see the truth of what this Asian master says.

Breathing exercises can greatly enhance awareness. Indeed, just becoming aware of your pattern of breathing is a good way to enter into prayer. But breathing exercises are not limited simply to becoming aware of your breathing. They also go beyond awareness to the control of breathing: they slow it down, deepen it, and make the rhythm of your inhalations and exhalations regular. Tony de Mello taught many different breathing and awareness exercises. He was once asked whether these kinds of exercises were merely preparations for prayer or were prayer itself. He answered that to enter into the present moment and be there is a great form of contemplative prayer; no one, he believed, could enter into that silence without in some way entering into contact with God, the very core of their being, the One who, as Saint Augustine said, "is more intimate to me than I am to myself" (*Confessions*, book 3, chapter 6).

Here are four exercises to prepare you for prayer.

EXERCISE 1:
AWARENESS OF YOUR BREATHING

This is a ten-minute exercise during which you observe your breathing but do not try to control it.

Find a comfortable place to sit, and a position in which you can keep your back straight and not feel the need to change your posture. Half close or close your eyes.

Now become aware of your breathing. Do not try to control it. Do not make an effort to breathe more slowly or deeply or regularly. If you breathe in a shallow way, keep breathing in a shallow way during the exercise. But be aware of it.

Become aware of the air as it enters your nostrils and brushes along the inside of your nostrils. Do not focus on the air as it enters your lungs. It is enough to become aware of the air as it enters your nostrils and makes its way up them.

- Is the air cold as it enters your nostrils? Is it warmer as it makes its way out?
- Does it feel like a caress?
- Does the air encounter resistance as it enters your nostrils?
- How fast does it pass through your nostrils?
- Does the same amount of air pass through each nostril?
- Where in your nostrils do you feel the air touch you most?
- Where does it touch you least?

As you do this exercise, you may be tempted to tighten your muscles. If you become aware of tension, simply let go of the tension; release any tenseness you feel into relaxation. You will also find your attention wandering. You will find yourself getting lost in distractions. This can make you tense or frustrated. But once you become aware of distractions, do not fight them in a worried or anxious way. Simply let them drop, and return to your awareness of breathing. Let your breathing be the anchor to which you return each time you get distracted.

EXERCISE 2: EMOTIONAL BREATHING

Once again, find a quiet place where you will not be disturbed. Adopt a comfortable posture with your back straight. To begin, simply become aware of your breathing.

Now take a further step beyond simple awareness of your breathing. Become aware of the presence of God in the air around you. As you breathe in and out, realize that God is present in this air. What do you feel when you notice God's presence in the air you breathe in and out? Do you feel awe? Surprise? Gratitude? Delight? Longing? Intimacy? Peace? Adoration?

Express whatever feeling you have by means of your breathing. Do not put the particular feeling you have into words, but into the way you breathe in and out. For example, if you feel gratitude, inhale deeply and completely as though you were literally taking in the goodness and giftedness of life with your every inhalation. And breathe out with a sense of returning the gift to the Giver, giving back the love you receive to the One who gives love to you with each breath.

As you inhale deeply, breathe positive feelings into your body and your whole being. As you deeply exhale, send forth any fears, tensions, and anxieties from your body.

EXERCISE 3:
THE WORLD OF SOUND

We described earlier in this chapter the judo technique that you can use to transform a distraction into a help for concentration. This technique is an important aid when it comes to sounds. We tend to divide things we hear into welcome and unwelcome sounds. As children we are told that certain sounds are disturbing and others are peace-inducing, and we go through life accepting this received wisdom. We learn that particular sounds are intrusive; for instance, the loud drone of a lawnmower outside, or the intermittent sound of music from the apartment next door. There are other sounds that we find welcoming: the sound of water lapping against the shore, a crackling fire, the peal of a church bell.

In reality, all sounds can help us to concentrate and be silent, with the exception of sounds that are so loud they damage our eardrums and give us headaches. Obviously, a harmful and earsplitting noise is something no one wants to hear. However, all other sounds are, in a surprising way, "sounds of silence." They are sounds that contain some slice of silence, or at least a call to silence. To check out the truth of this claim, do the following ten-minute exercise:

Settle into a comfortable posture and quiet yourself by breathing slowly, regularly, and deeply for a few minutes. Close your eyes and listen to all the sounds around you, beginning with the sounds farthest away: the sound of traffic outside, of people's voices on the street, an airplane overhead, a bird singing, a dog barking.

Now become aware of sounds nearer to you, within your house or in your room: a curtain rustling in the breeze, a clock ticking, a computer humming.

Next focus on the sounds *inside* you: the sound of your breath as you inhale and exhale, the sound of your heart beating, the rumbling of your stomach.

Finally, listen to all sounds—inside and outside—without giving them a name, without calling them honking horns or footsteps or purring machines. Simply listen to all these sounds as though they formed a single unified sound.

If you do this exercise a few times, you will begin to realize that sounds are not things you have to block out or shun or ignore. You can actually use sounds as avenues toward silence. Paradoxically, sounds can lead you into quiet.

EXERCISE 4:
CONTROLLED DEEP BREATHING

The focus of the following ten-minute exercise is not to become aware of your breathing, but to control and modulate it.

Sit down in a comfortable place, with your back straight. Now begin to inhale slowly and deeply through your nostrils. Keep your mouth closed. Feel the air as it enters up through your nostrils and then goes down through your body into your lungs. Put your hand on your stomach and feel it expand outward as the air moves downward. Do not tighten the muscles of your stomach. Keep them relaxed, and your stomach will expand better.

Keeping your hand on your stomach, hold your breath for a moment. Then exhale slowly and deeply with a long continuous breath. Press your stomach gently with your hand to help force out the air inside. As you do so, make sure to keep your chest and ribcage relaxed.

Variation: Once you become used to inhaling and exhaling slowly and deeply, move on to this slight variation: Put your hand on your abdomen as you inhale, and feel your abdomen moving outward as the air enters your lungs. Allow your chest to lift slightly. Keep your abdomen relaxed. As you exhale, press your hand slightly against your abdomen, and utter a long sigh to accompany your exhalation.

REVIEW

Stories. Reread the story of Cain and Abel and Poe's story "The Purloined Letter." How does the story of Cain and Abel relate to your relationship with God? As you reflect upon the story of the stolen letter, does it trigger any realization that there may be something obvious in your life that you have lost sight of?

Key phrase. *Your breathing is your greatest friend.* "And God breathed into his nostrils the breath of life; and the man became a living being" (Gen 2:7). Genesis tells us that we are shaped from the dust and clay of the earth, molded by God like a potter molds a vase. And then God breathes into our nostrils the breath (Hebrew: *ruach*) of life. God does not breathe into the nostrils of any other creature. This intimate gesture marks us apart from everything else on earth. No animal is privy to such a special divine privilege. While our "clay" nature puts us on a par with the material elements in creation, the "breath of life" gives us a higher and spiritual identity.

Breath or wind is invisible. We cannot see it with our eyes or fix it with our gaze. It is immaterial and invisible. This breath is what animates us and makes us alive.

The Hebrew word *ruach* is not only the word for "breath" or "wind"; it is also the word for the Spirit. For its part, the English word *spirit*, derives from the word for breath and breathing: from the Latin noun *spiritus*, which means "breath."

The breath that gives life to us is not a one-time gift. We do not breathe just at the beginning of life, but all through life. We receive the gift of air into our lungs constantly. The oxygen we receive with every inhalation is carried to every part of the body, and with every exhalation, we release carbon dioxide. The gift of breath is grossly underestimated. We rarely reflect that—beyond life itself—intelligence as well is impossible without breathing. Without breath there would be no food, no families, no forests, no trees, no work, no buildings, no cities, no nations—nothing.

But although all of us breathe, few of us breathe in a wholesome way. In Genesis, God breathes into the nostrils to give the breath of life. Many of us breathe through the mouth; we would be healthier if we followed God's example and always breathed through the nostrils. When it comes to breathing, depth is also important: we benefit from breathing deeply. In addition, a slower rate of breathing induces calm and tranquility. Rhythm too is a vital aspect of breathing; consistent regularity in breathing and an even alternation between inhalation and exhalation attune us to the rhythm of the heart and other bodily organs. The rhythm, rate, and depth of our breathing have a strong impact on our consciousness. For instance, by breathing deeply and slowly we become calmer, and we decrease stress and anxiety.

Breathing is your greatest friend because "we are how we breathe." In fact, the regulation of the breath plays a pivotal role in the spiritual journey. If we tune into the appropriate rhythm in our breathing, we can even harmonize our personal breathing with the very vibration of the universe.

Practical exercises. We have presented several exercises in this chapter. They are not simply one-off exercises, but exercises that are useful to do all during your journey of prayer. They can be done on their own, or they can be used as preparation for prayer.

CHAPTER THREE

Ways of Praying

Henri Nouwen (1932–96) was one of the most popular spiritual guides of the twentieth century. He wrote many bestselling books on spirituality. After teaching at Yale, Notre Dame, and Harvard, Nouwen took a surprise move "down" the career ladder by becoming an assistant at a L'Arche community for disabled people near Toronto, Canada. As an intellectual who loved teaching and was used to audiences who admired him, Nouwen found this new direction to be intensely challenging. He was assigned to take care of Adam, a young man who was unable to speak or move without help, and who had frequent seizures. This assignment terrified Nouwen more than anything else he had ever done. But slowly he and Adam made a connection. In the process, Nouwen began to get a sense of what it must be like for God to relate to us: to our woundedness, our lack of coordination, our severe handicaps, our minimal response to God's immense love. (See Henri Nouwen, *Adam: God's Beloved*, Maryknoll, NY: Orbis, 1997.)

Nouwen was sustained in his work by a deep prayer life. Each day he sat, knelt, or lay prostrate before the tabernacle. Nouwen wanted God's love to flood his heart daily, so that every word and gesture of his would be full of grace and unction. Yet, although prayer was at the heart of his life, he found it extremely difficult to be still. He was a man of great energy, always doing things. People who had heard about this famous contemplative were often taken aback when they actually saw him at prayer: he could not stop fidgeting, moving, and tapping his legs. One woman who observed Nouwen closely was initially shocked at his restlessness and constant movement. But over time she began to realize that only his body was in motion; his spirit was totally focused on God.

It is always reassuring to discover that someone prays and to see them at prayer, even if their prayer is unconventional, as was Nouwen's. Most people hardly share at all about their prayer, especially priests, who are supposedly "professional" pray-ers.

Tony de Mello once made a helpful analogy between prayer and eating. He said that if you go to a restaurant and the waiter gives you the menu to eat, you will not get any real nourishment. Nobody wants to eat the menu; they want food. When you look at a menu and see the word *chicken*, you want to eat the chicken, not the word. We spend a lot of time *talking* about God, but what people really hunger after is the *experience* of God. They are fed up of being offered menus; they want to eat the food.

Prayer is not simply an added extra in Christianity. Saint Gregory of Nazianzen (329–90 AD) said, "We must remember God more often than we draw breath" (*Oratio theologica prima*, I, 4). No wonder Jesus gave energy and time to teaching people how to pray: *prayer is oxygen for the soul*. If you stop breathing, you stop living. If you stop praying, your soul dies. Prayer is like a good meal. Without food, you do not grow; in fact, sooner or later you stop living. Without prayer, your spirit shrivels up and dies. Prayer transforms your life, making difficult things easy. It helps you overcome apparently insurmountable obstacles. In the words of Saint John Chrysostom (347–407 AD): "Nothing is equal to prayer; for what is impossible it makes possible, what is difficult, easy" (*De Anna sermones* 4, 5).

A lot of people draw a blank when it comes to prayer. They would like to pray, but they simply have no idea how to approach prayer. But the truth is that prayer is as natural as breathing. The

French mystic Thérèse of Lisieux proclaimed, "For me, prayer is an aspiration of the heart, it is a simple glance directed to heaven, it is a cry of gratitude and love in the midst of trial as well as joy" (*Story of a Soul*, trans. John Clarke, Washington, DC: ICS Publications, 1976, p. 242). Here is an even simpler definition: *prayer is the conversation of the heart with God.* There are many, many different ways to pray. And there is a vast array of techniques to help enter into prayer: breathing, relaxation, silence, imagination, mantras, and phrases from scripture.

But why should we pray? There are many good reasons. Prayer helps us fall in love with God and others, and responds to that deep hunger inside our hearts for real food. Prayer shows us who we are in our deepest being. It gets us in touch (or back in touch) with the "why" of our lives, and attunes us to what is really important. Prayer centers us and unifies us in the face of the messiness and fragmentation of life.

When it comes to any activity in life—whether it is swimming, studying, playing golf, or cooking—it is easiest if you follow certain basic guidelines. You cannot swing a golf club any old way you feel like doing it; you have to spend time acquiring the skill. And the reason why you cannot do it any old way that you want to is because, despite their different styles, all tour golfers have fundamentally a similar swing: 95 percent of each one's backswing, position at impact, and follow-through is the same as the others'. This is why beginners often model themselves on outstanding players; for example, they try to swing a golf club like Jack Nicklaus.

When it comes to finding a model for speaking with God, there are two outstanding prayers that have touched millions of people. The first, with its message of unconditional love, contains the blueprint for a new social order, for a harmonious way of living with each other in our globalized world. With the world now electronically connected, it is possible to create worldwide networks of instantaneous communication, not only in work and technology, but also in prayer and in loving. And despite the split between Catholics and Protestants with the Reformation, all Christian denominations look back for inspiration to the stirring figure of Saint Francis of Assisi—and to the luminous prayer that bears his name.

The exercise below will help you make this prayer into a real conversation with God. But first: If the following version is not familiar to you and becomes a distraction, then try this exercise using the version of the prayer with which you are most comfortable.

EXERCISE 1:
THE PRAYER OF SAINT FRANCIS AS REFLECTIVE PRAYER

Find a quiet place where you are unlikely to be disturbed. Sit in a comfortable position. Become aware of how you are breathing. Gently slow down the pace of your breath, drawing each breath more deeply inside yourself. Close your eyes if it helps you shut out distracting sights. But if closing your eyes makes you lose the train of your thoughts or induces sleepiness, keep your eyes open and focus them on a special object, such as a candle or an icon. Now recite the words of the Prayer of Saint Francis quietly to yourself, as you slowly breathe in and out.

> Lord, make me a channel of your peace;
> where there is hatred, may I bring love;
> where there is wrong, may I bring the spirit of forgiveness;
> where there is discord, may I bring harmony;
> where there is error, may I bring truth;
> where there is doubt, may I bring faith;
> where there is despair, may I bring hope;
> where there are shadows, may I bring light;
> where there is sadness, may I bring joy.

Lord, grant that I may seek rather to comfort than to be
    comforted;
to understand, than to be understood;
to love, than to be loved.
For it is by self-forgetting that one finds.
It is by forgiving that one is forgiven.
It is by dying that one awakens to eternal life. Amen.

Now start this prayer again, this time stopping when you arrive
at a word or phrase that draws you or grips you. Let us suppose that
the word *Lord*, the very opening of the prayer, really attracts you.
Pause at this word and begin to repeat it over and over again:
Lord...Lord...Lord. Let the word sink into you. Do not try to reflect
on the word, but simply repeat it in your heart, allowing it to wash
over you like the waves of the ocean. And when you have immersed
your spirit in this word long enough, you will find yourself either
wanting to say something to God or else being content to remain
silent and happy in God's presence, filled with the power and peace
this word brings you.

If this particular word of the prayer touches you in a particular way, and you may find yourself speaking from your heart like this:
*Lord...Lord...Lord...*Are you really "Lord"? Can I trust you? I
want to trust you with my life, but it is so hard for me. I'm so used
to being in control and calling the shots. It is hard to let go, to
loosen my grip. Please help me to trust!

Or the next words may resonate in a deep way. You may say
something like: *Make me a channel of your peace...a channel...channel...of*
*peace...peace...*Lord, I want to be a channel. I want to empty myself
of my ego and pride. Please use me. Please act through me. For your
purposes, and not for mine. And help me be at peace. Help me calm
the inner turmoil, the anxiety I so often feel. Give me peace. Please
don't let me drift into sleep and vegetation...

Go through the whole prayer like this, slowly, pausing whenever you feel drawn by a words or words, repeating those words, savoring them, and then responding personally to God out of this sense of being touched.

As an example and a help to your own prayer, we offer a few more lines to enable you to see concretely what it means to relish and savor the words of this magnificent prayer. However, when you actually do this exercise yourself, please do not feel you have to complete the whole prayer. The purpose is not to rush to the finish line of the Prayer of Saint Francis, but to enter into loving communication with God, to whom the prayer is addressed. You may find that you are gripped for your whole prayer time by just one or two phrases, and that is absolutely fine. Stay with whatever leads you to speak lovingly to God, as long as you can do so without distraction. Once you get distracted, move on to the next phrase that appeals to you.

*Where there is hatred, may I bring love...bring love...love...*Lord, help me transform hatred into love. And please open a space of love in my own heart, a love that lasts, a love that is fruitful, a love that reaches out in kind words and touching gestures. May I bring love, may I live love, may I one day be Love...

*Where there is wrong, may I bring the spirit of forgiveness...forgiveness ...forgiveness...*Lord, I don't want to hold on to anger or resentment. I want to forgive, but it's not easy. Move my heart to forgive. I cannot do it by myself. It is your gift. Give me your gift. Help me to forgive...

*Where there is discord, may I bring harmony...discord to harmony...harmony ...*Lord, help me find harmony, help me become attuned to you, help me connect with all that is generous and loving and nurturing in the world.

THE METHOD BEHIND THIS PRAYER

You may have noticed that we invited you to follow a particular method in praying the Prayer of Saint Francis. This method has three steps: (1) reciting and repeating, (2) saturating and savoring, and (3) responding personally and resting prayerfully. You begin by reciting in your heart the word or words in the passage that appeal to you, repeating the word or phrase over and over again. In the second phase, you savor and relish the words: you saturate your heart with these words by simple repetition. And when you feel satiated, you move to the third step. This is the stage at which "prayer" in the strict sense of the word begins. You speak spontaneously out of the feelings the words evoke in your heart, or else you stay silently and lovingly in God's presence, filled with the grace of those words.

You can follow this three-step method with any prayer, as well as with any of your favorite passages from the Bible. Take a passage from scripture with which you are already familiar, and read through it slowly, pausing when you arrive at a phrase whose beauty attracts you. Stop at that word or phrase. Repeat it to yourself until you absorb it into your heart and it really becomes part of you. When you are filled and satiated, spontaneously speak from your heart to God, or stay lovingly and quietly in the Lord's presence, continuing to savor the power of the words that fill your heart. Remain with this third and last phase of the prayer as long as you can do so without being distracted. If you become distracted, start the whole process again, reading further until another word or phrase claims your attention.

If you are not accustomed to praying with your heart (and you are not alone here!), this form of prayer is wonderfully transformative. This is because it provides a role both for your head and your heart. It leads you ultimately to your heart, but it goes by way of the mind, so that the intellect is not neglected or left unoccupied. Your head has something to do in the initial two phases when you recite/repeat and saturate/savor. But the manner of praying nudges you gently into your heart-space from the beginning. It moves you toward simplicity and toward your feelings and affections.

EXERCISE 2:
THE OUR FATHER AS VOCAL PRAYER

In the last exercise we took the Prayer of Saint Francis as our theme for prayer, but we approached it in a leisurely and reflective manner, stopping at words and phrases that were especially gripping. There was no pressure to finish the prayer. The goal was not to recite the prayer aloud or try to complete it within a short period of time, but to dwell on certain words and phrases. The aim was to let the words of the prayer resonate inside, so as to lead either to a prayerful response to God or to a loving silence in God's presence.

Now we turn to the Our Father as vocal prayer, reciting it aloud or simply whispering the words. What counts in vocal prayer is not the number of prayers we say or the length of the prayers, but the attention and devotion with which we recite them. It is quality not quantity that makes the difference. We live in a world that is impressed by quantity: by statistics, by the size of a house or the price of a car, by the number of dollars you take home each week. But in prayer, it is quality that counts. And this applies to vocal prayer as well. In fact, Jesus condemned those who put on a big show or a pretense by making long prayers (Matt 6:7). And when you think of it, wouldn't a good friend be happier to hear you say a few words full of emotion, instead of a thousand words of empty chatter? In the same way, God prefers one loving phrase to a thousand without any feeling or fervor. It is not the number of words that are important, but the passion and feeling of the one who says them. It is no use saying something with your lips unless you feel it in your soul. As King Claudius sadly realizes in Shakespeare's *Hamlet*:

> My words fly up, my thoughts remain below:
> Words without thoughts never to heaven go.

Before starting to recite the Our Father, make sure you are in a comfortable posture with your back straight. Notice how you are breathing. Start breathing slowly, regularly, and deeply for a few minutes to calm your spirit—and body. Become aware that you are in the presence of God. In God, you live and move and have your being.

Start reciting the words of the Lord's Prayer with full attention. This means two things: first, be fully aware of the words you are uttering; and second, be fully aware of the Person to whom you are speaking. Here we use a slightly different wording from normal in order to awaken you to some of the startling freshness of this prayer. But if you find the traditional wording more helpful, please stay with it. Choose whichever helps you pray best.

> Our Father in heaven, may your name be held holy. May your kingdom come. May your loving plan be followed on earth as it is in heaven. Give us this day our daily nourishment. Forgive us what we owe as we forgive those who owe to us. Avert temptations from us, and save us from the Evil One.

Speak these words slowly and from the fullness of your heart. If you find your attention wandering at any point, return to the word where you became distracted and repeat it until you can pronounce the word with perfect attention. Be as intentional as possible about the meaning of the words. Make the meaning of the words your own by saying them with as much eagerness and feeling as you can, and keeping in mind that you are not saying these words to just anyone, but to the God of the universe. Gather all your attention and focus it on God and on what you are saying to God.

Although millions of people recite the words of the Lord's Prayer, no two people say it in exactly the same manner. If you say this prayer from your heart, it will be *your* prayer. It will be utterly unique, bearing the distinctive stamp of your personality and character. It will be your unmistakable act of praise and worship.

Perfect attention is crucial when it comes to vocal prayer. In her book *Waiting for God*, the French mystic Simone Weil underlined the importance of attention. To explain what attention meant for her, she told the old Eskimo tale about the origin of light. There was a blackbird that lived in the eternal night. It was unable to find food. So with all the energy of its being, it desired the light. Lo and behold, the earth lit up. Simone Weil understood from this story the power of true desire. If the desire for light is perfectly focused upon light, it will be so powerful that it will produce light. You must desire light with perfect attention, and light will truly flood your heart. You must desire God with perfect attention, and God will inundate your heart with the fullness of presence. If you direct your gaze solely toward God during prayer, then God's love will enter your heart, shine through you, and illuminate everything in you and around you. By attending to God, by focusing your attention exclusively on God, you will transform your world.

REVIEW

Stories. Recall the story of the importance of prayer for Henri Nouwen. Relating Nouwen's story to yourself, how important would you like prayer to be in your life? Even if we are self-confident in other areas, we are all prone to great self-doubt when it comes to prayer. For many people, the most difficult thing of all is actually starting. It is like that moment when we stand at the edge of a cold swimming pool, afraid to jump in. We know that once we are in the water we will enjoy it, but actually getting in can be incredibly difficult. Or when we think of praying, we suddenly remember a host of other things that need to be done. Or perhaps we cannot escape the sinking feeling that prayer is going to be a difficult slog, hard work, with our mind wandering all over the place and filled with distractions. And then we invariably compare ourselves unfavorably with others: we imagine that others can pray much better than we ever could.

We can assure you that most people we know feel hesitant and uncertain when it comes to prayer. Everyone finds that something or other gets in the way of the desire to pray. Everyone feels that others can pray more easily. Everyone feels that he or she is simply not cut out for this intimidating thing called "prayer." But anyone who does make the effort to pray will discover that life changes in a big way as a result. Friends are usually the first to notice in you a new sense of peace, a release from tension, a joy in the simple things of life. Prayer heals your life, gives you harmony and balance, and opens up a space where God can touch you in an unexpectedly beautiful way.

It is important to start small, but think big. Don't undertake too much at the beginning. Choose a time and a place to pray each day, and then ease yourself gently into a rhythm. Start with five or ten minutes. As you become accustomed to it, you can gradually lengthen your daily period of prayer. After a month you will find yourself praying for longer periods. But don't wait until you feel like praying to begin praying: if we only prayed when we felt like it, most of us would hardly pray at all! And don't wait until you are less busy to start praying, you will always have other things to do. The only way to begin praying is to get down to doing it. Don't wait until tomorrow to start. Don't postpone it until an emergency. Now is the time!

The second story was the Eskimo tale about the origin of

light. It told of the intense longing of the blackbird for light. The power of desire puts things within our grasp.

Key phrases. *Prayer is oxygen for the soul,* and *prayer is the conversation of the heart with God.* Prayer is also an antidote to fear. You truly pray when you raise your whole being to God. In prayer, you find the strength to love and to awaken love in others. Only through coming to know God in prayer will you know what love is and how to love. You will not always feel like praying; something inside often holds us back. Encourage yourself at those hesitant moments with thoughts of God's love, and of how easy it is to talk to the Lord. The hesitation and resistance are all on your side, not on God's. The passion and desire for intimacy are above all on God's side. This realization will give you new courage and help you to persevere.

To help you find the way to pray that works best for you, we will continue to offer you a number of different ways of praying during the course of this book. Try them, experiment with them, and you will discover which ways suit you best. These methods can inspire you to go beyond saying prayers in a mechanical way and help you experience prayer as the expression of a loving relationship with God. They can challenge you to experiment with ways of praying that you may have never dreamed of before. They will help you find the way you pray best, the way you best communicate with God. How you pray best may change many times in the course of a lifetime. Indeed, it may change in the course of a particular day: you may find yourself reciting prayers when you wake up in the morning, whereas in the evening you may be content simply to sit in front of an icon or cross and just look.

Some people find God most easily in the "mirror" of others. And so the prayer of those people is often filled with the presence of family and friends. Other people find God's presence in nature. They like praying on mountaintops or seashores, or, if they cannot get there, they transport themselves in imagination to a place of beauty while they pray.

How often should you pray? As often as you can. In fact, God invites you to pray unceasingly. This does not mean retiring to the silence of a monastery. Instead, it is a matter of punctuating your day with the remembrance of God. It means speaking to God in all your activities. Nothing highbrow or complicated: simple things like telling God how your life is going, and sharing your joys and frustrations. Peace will be your reward.

Practical exercises. We offered two different ways of praying: the Prayer of Saint Francis as reflective prayer, and the Our Father as vocal prayer. These two ways of praying can also be used with favorite passages from scripture and can be applied when using traditional prayers as well.

CHAPTER FOUR

Finding a Loving God

God regularly gets blamed for what's bad in life. We even use the expression "act of God" for natural disasters such as volcanic eruptions, floods, and earthquakes. God gets little credit for the many things that go right. But then, God does not have a particularly good PR agency, because organized religion is not always a winning advertisement for God. The Irish writer Brian Moore opens one of his early stories with the following arresting phrase: "In the beginning was the word, and the word was NO!" Many people can resonate with this negativity when it comes to religion. They find it difficult to see a loving God at the heart of organized religion. This and other difficulties lead to a deepening distance. Because of bad experiences at home, school, or church, people get the message that God is a tough and demanding taskmaster. It is not surprising that they want to keep as far away from God as possible.

BAD UNCLE GEORGE

The British Jesuit Gerard Hughes spent years working as a college chaplain. He listened to countless students who had difficulties with their Catholic faith. Slowly he began to piece together the features common to their image of God. It was a distorted image of God, to say the least. In his book *The God of Surprises*, he puts together the typical college "identikit picture" of God—it is sobering reading. The parents of these young people invariably presented God as a friendly, powerful figure who was personally interested in their lives. He was a kind of benevolent family relative. But then one day they took their child to visit "Good Old Uncle George," as Hughes calls him. Somehow the child could not summon up the same enthusiasm about this uncle that its parents had: there was something gruff and unfriendly about him. As the visit to Uncle George was about to finish, this bearded and intimidating man turned to the child and made it clear in no uncertain terms that he expected a weekly visit. If not, the kid would be taken to the basement of his mansion for punishment. To demonstrate the nature of the punishment, he led the child down a dark stairs. The temperature grew suddenly hotter. Terrible screams could be heard from below. Uncle George opened a steel door to show a hellish vision of burning furnaces flanked by demons, ready to throw in anyone who failed to turn up for the weekly visit to his home. After that, he brought the child back upstairs. The parents smiled and thanked Uncle George for the visit. As they brought the child home, the mother turned and asked, "Don't you absolutely love Uncle George with all your mind and heart and soul and strength?" And although the child hated this frightful uncle, it felt compelled to answer "yes" so as not to be added to the number of those thrown into the blazing fiery furnace.

We have had conversations with people who confess that they are simply unable to believe in God. As a rule they are well-meaning people. In fact, many are genuine seekers. When we ask them what they mean by the word *God*, they describe him in myriad ways, ranging from a disinterested Creator to an impersonal force. They are left cold by the notion of God. They find no evidence that God has a personal interest in them. They have not been touched.

The truth is that God knows you even if you do not know God. *God believes in you more than you believe in yourself.* God loves you even if you do not know God and so do not love God. A father does not stop being a father when a son is ignorant. A mother does not cease being a mother when a daughter is bad. A father tries to teach an ignorant son. A mother tries to correct a bad daughter, weeps tears for the child, and forgives her failings. And is God the Father less kind than a human father or a human mother? God loves each person as if that person were the only person in the world. God's plan is to gather everyone into unity, so that all human beings may be brothers and sisters of each other, and children of the one Father. God has no favorites: God chooses some, only to reach the rest.

BLINDNESS

Who is this great God then? To answer this question, let us tell you a wonderful Sufi story about some blind scouts who were sent to get information about an enormous creature that was just outside their town. Although the scouts did not know it, this creature was in reality an elephant. Having no idea about the shape of an elephant, they went up to it and began to touch different parts of the animal. Each scout touched only one part, so each learned something different. When they returned to their superiors, the scouts were asked to describe the elephant. The scout that had felt the elephant's ear said that the elephant was large and round, like a rough rug. But the scout who had touched the trunk promptly disagreed. He claimed that the elephant was long and straight and powerful, like a hollow pipe. However the scout that had touched the legs of the elephant said it was stately and firm, like four enormous pillars. Their bosses were left in complete confusion. Although each scout spoke with certainty, everyone's evidence was contradictory. Each scout had only a fragment of truth. No one had the complete picture. And everyone took the part for the whole.

What we imagine about God also falls far short of the full picture. We cannot reach God with our mind. God is infinitely beyond anything we can imagine. God cannot be known because God is a mystery. Thomas Aquinas stated that every time we say something about God, we must both deny it and exaggerate it beyond recognition. For instance, if we say, "God is good," we also must deny it by saying, "but God is not good in the manner that human beings are good," and then we have to add, "God is good in an indescribable way, with a goodness utterly beyond anything we can imagine."

Attempts to describe God are like the effort to describe a color to someone who was born blind. Suppose a blind man asks you one day what the color green is like, and you say it is smooth like satin. The next day another blind man asks you the same question, and you reply that it is like a murmuring breeze. The following afternoon you come across the two men having a big argument. One is shouting, "It is smooth like satin," and the other is screaming, "No, it is like a murmuring breeze." In fact, they have no idea what they are really arguing about.

Even though it is beyond the power of the human mind to conceive God, Christianity gives us a helpful picture. God turns out to be much more humane than we are. What does God impose on human beings? An impossible burden? A million rules and laws? No. Just one law, which reflects God in its perfect simplicity: "Love God with your whole self, and love your neighbor as yourself." That's it.

The God of Jesus Christ also gives us the means to become gods ourselves. The one who does what Jesus says and who believes in what he teaches will climb the divine mountain and become a child of God. What Jesus teaches can be summed up in three high-energy "routes" to fullness that strengthen you and enable you to draw goodness into your life: love God with all your being, love your neighbor, and love yourself.

EXERCISE 1: SEEING A LOVING GOD

Jesus is the perfect image of the Father. In this meditation, to discover what God is like, we look at Jesus as he hangs from the cross. In action movies, the hero overcomes the bad guys with super-human strength and courage. But when evil gathers around Jesus, and some of his followers urge him to lead a rebellion against the Romans, he does not resort to violent means to conquer his enemies. Instead, he meekly allows himself to be crucified. Though Jesus disappoints human expectations by submitting to death, in another way he exceeds them, because after undergoing death, Jesus rises.

First, read the following Gospel passage:

> *When they came to the place called the Skull, there they crucified him, along with the criminals—one on his right, the other on his left. Jesus said, "Father, forgive them, for they do not know what they are doing."...One of the criminals who hung there hurled insults at him: "Aren't you the Christ? Save yourself and us!" But the other criminal rebuked him. "Don't you fear God," he said, "since you are under the same sentence? We are punished justly, for we are getting what our deeds deserve. But this man has done nothing wrong." Then he said, "Jesus, remember me when you come into your kingdom." Jesus answered him, "I tell you the truth, today you will be with me in paradise."* (Luke 23:33–34, 39–43)

Gather and recollect yourself, using an awareness exercise to prepare you for this period of prayer.

First, picture the overall scene. The hill of Calvary...Is it far outside Jerusalem? What is the weather like? Are there many people gathered there? What do you hear them say? How many soldiers are there? What do the three crosses look like? Now, let the scene itself come alive:

Look at Jesus on the cross, and look at the two criminals hanging at either side of him. Look at the bruises, swellings, cuts, and blood where his body has been scourged. Does the weight of his body push him forward? Downward? Look at the knot of thorns that pierce his head. Notice his face. Is it swollen? Is there blood trickling down? Is there dust sticking to his face after his repeated falls on the way here? Where are you in this scene? What are you doing? Who is around you?

Listen as Jesus speaks for the first time and says these unforgettable words: "Father, forgive them, for they do not know what they are doing." Notice the expression on his face as he makes this prayer aloud to the Father. Did you expect Jesus to say something like this? Can others hear these words of Jesus? If so, what effect do they have on his hearers? How do they affect you?

Listen to the wrongdoer on the next cross hurling insults at Jesus. How does Jesus react? What do you feel when you hear these insults? Do you want to take any action? Compare these insulting words to those of the other man, who attempts to restrain him and speaks out in Jesus' defense. Listen to his tone of voice as he pleads, "Jesus, remember me when you come into your kingdom." Look at the expression on Jesus' face as he replies, "I tell you the truth, today you will be with me in paradise." What effect do these words have on the man? Is anyone else able to hear these words of Jesus? What impression does this exchange make on you?

Now Jesus turns to you. What is his expression like? Does he say anything to you? What are you feeling? What do you want to say to him?

Pray for a while to Jesus, thanking him for the new things you have learned about God through spending this time in his company.

GOD'S EMBRACE

A young man, recently married, spent a few days in prayer, guided by a spiritual master. The young man was a good and conscientious Christian, but he was unable to feel God's love in his heart. His religion was a matter of "shoulds," and it was all in his head. The spiritual guide invited the young man to imagine God holding him in a warm embrace. For two days he dutifully tried, but he simply could not picture God in this way. On the final day he felt down and despondent, and was about to give up in frustration. Then he suddenly pictured his wife, and how she embraced him. At that moment the penny dropped, he got the insight, and he was flooded with joy as he realized that God loved him as tenderly as his wife.

Can you picture a loving God? It can be extremely difficult if you have grown up with an image of a harsh God, a God who punishes you severely for the least transgression. It can also be difficult if you have an image of a disinterested God.

Can you imagine Jesus hugging you? If you see God as a prison warden, then God will not be inclined to embrace you. If you see God as a strict teacher, you won't want God to come too close. Yet if you begin to see that God loves you like the person closest to you does, this will make a big difference. It is crucial to link God's love with human love. If you have been embraced and hugged by others, you can dare to believe that God's love is at least as full and generous as this human love.

Your image of God decides how much you let God into your life. If your image of God is off-putting, the last thing you will want is for God to draw near to you. But if you can link your picture of God to your impression of the kindest people you know, the kind of people for whom you feel deep affection, you will be willing to welcome God into your heart.

That young man made big progress once he could imagine God embracing him. There is great healing power in the visualization of God's love. If you can picture God's love in a concrete way, you will be able to abandon destructive images and replace them with constructive and unifying ones. And soon your life will mirror this constructive love. You will begin to act out of love instead of less helpful dispositions. Your sense of self-worth will grow. God says, "Can a mother forget the baby at her breast and have no compassion on the child she has borne? Though she may forget, I will not forget you!" (Isa 49:15, NIV).

In order to convey the extraordinary generosity of God's unconditional love, Tony de Mello related the following poignant experience from his own life. To test and provoke his mother, he once asked her how she would feel if he left the priesthood and got married. With a sad look in her eyes, she replied, "I would feel deep disappointment. But your wife would be my daughter." He concluded, "I believe that God loves me exactly like that, with no conditions, no strings attached."

EXERCISE 2: THE JESUS PRAYER

According to one ancient tradition, the good thief hanging next to Jesus was the first to pronounce the words of what we today call the Jesus Prayer. Tony de Mello remarked that God's name is also invoked in Hinduism, where there is a prayer similar to the Jesus Prayer, called the "Remembrance of the Name." Mahatma Gandhi said he had overcome all his fears through incessantly repeating God's name. The use of God's name in prayer can change our lives. It can also change our world. It holds more than immense power: it contains infinite power.

The Jesus Prayer invokes the name of Jesus, which for Christians is the name above all names, the power above all powers. In the Bible, there is nothing trivial or incidental about a person's name. In fact, a name stands for the full person; a name manifests someone's complete character. God's name, then, is not a mere collection of letters or syllables: instead it is the very presence and nature of God.

Jesus is the living center of the universe. He is everywhere, extending beyond all physical and material boundaries. He is accessible wherever you are. The only way you can become separate from him is by doubting that you can connect. Believe that you can tune into Jesus, and you will activate your connection with him.

Initially, it is best to spend at most ten to fifteen minutes praying the Jesus Prayer. There are different forms of this prayer, but at its simplest, it consists of the single word *Jesus*. Adopt a posture that is both comfortable and conducive to reverence: sit with your back straight, or stand, or kneel. Keep your eyes closed or half-closed. Prepare yourself for this invocation by asking the Holy Spirit to give you the unction to pronounce the name of Jesus with desire and love.

If you have access to a chapel or oratory, you may find it helpful to go there and sit in front of a tabernacle, a Bible, or a sacred image. Otherwise try to picture Jesus in your imagination. In what way does your heart see him? As a helpless baby...a young boy in the Temple...an adolescent...the charismatic preacher, teacher, and healer...the Crucified One...the Risen Lord...?

Where do you see Jesus? Right next to you? In the midst of a Gospel scene? Or perhaps you do not see him, but feel his presence within your heart.

Now, as you breathe in and out, pronounce the name of Jesus at a rhythm that brings you peace. For instance, you may say "Jesus" each time you inhale and "Jesus" each time you exhale. Or you may pronounce the first syllable as you breathe in and the second syllable as you breathe out. Or you may decide to pronounce the name of Jesus only every third breath. The important thing is to find a natural rhythm that allows you to pray in a relaxed, reverent, and attentive way.

If you feel drained at repeating the name of Jesus, pause for a few moments before starting to recite it again.

As you become accustomed to pronouncing the name, activate different feelings and dispositions as you say it. Without saying the words *thank you*, pour a spirit of gratitude into the way you say the name Jesus. Let this feeling of gratitude fill your being as you recite his name.

After a while, take up another attitude, this time adoration. As you recite the name Jesus, pronounce it with the intense admiration of adoration, with the profound devotion and total surrender that characterize adoration. Continue to say Jesus in worship of the One who surrounds you and encompasses you. Then move on to other attitudes and feelings: longing, trust, serenity, repentance...

Finally, listen in your imagination as Jesus says *your* name. Jesus knows you as no one else does, and he says your name as no one else can. How does he say your name? What happens to you when you hear him pronounce your name?

As you finish, thank the Lord for the way he has touched you during this time of prayer.

As we repeat the name of Jesus, it seeps into our very being, and steadily transforms us.

REVIEW

Stories. There were three main stories in this chapter: "Bad Uncle George," the three blind scouts and the elephant, and the young man who could not imagine Jesus embracing him. Take some time to mull over these stories. Dostoevsky once observed that it is all too easy to go through life without ever finding yourself in yourself. These stories will shed light on your life. They will open you up to the riches of your inner world.

Key phrase. *God believes in you more than you believe in yourself.* There are so many possibilities lying dormant inside you. It is only in the warmth of love that these possibilities come to life. You can easily get distracted by false ways of nourishing your hunger for love. You can become a workaholic, get fixated by success, or restlessly search for the ideal partner in your life. But if you enter your heart, love will come to your door and break through the barriers of self-loathing and egoism. When you experience God's love, you will begin to discover new dimensions of your being. This perfect love will cast out fear and transfigure you with its emotional flame.

Practical exercises. In this chapter, you meditated on Jesus on the cross and learned to pray the Jesus Prayer. These two meditations are particularly powerful, because their focus is Jesus. On the cross, Jesus removes the negative energy of guilt, shame, stress, and worry. The power of the cross is disarming: its vulnerability makes us strong; its nails make us free. The recital of the name of Jesus heals our bodies and our souls. It changes our personal history.

CHAPTER FIVE

Who Am I?

The real issue for many of us is not so much God, or at least not *first* of all God, but ourselves. The question is not "who is God?" Instead, the burning question is "who am I?" Before people can launch fruitfully into the spiritual journey, they need the basic security of knowing who they are. They need to enjoy being human before they can happily search for the divine. They need to unblock their own hurts before they can trust enough to open to God. Prior to discovering the liberating truth of the divine, they need to find the liberating truth of who they themselves are.

As much as 95 percent of your problems are not spiritual. So if you want your journey into faith to bear real fruit, your own humanity needs to grow and ripen first. Looking back on the conversations we have had with so many spiritual searchers, we notice a particular pattern to them. The starting point of these conversations is usually not explicitly religious at all. Initially, people come to talk to us about other concerns. They begin by sharing the difficulties they experience in relationships, families, careers; they ask for advice and a listening ear as they face major life decisions.

TWO SELVES

Tony de Mello often told the unforgettable story of the eagle who suffered from a mistaken identity. The story goes like this: A man discovered a large egg on a clump of grass. He was worried the bird inside would never hatch, so he carried it to a farmyard and put it in a hen's nest. In time, a large eaglet hatched, alongside a brood of tiny chickens. As it grew up, it followed the habits of the chickens around it, clucking and cackling, pecking at the clay to unearth worms. Now and then it would flap its wings and fly for a few feet before falling to the ground again. Time passed. The eagle that always thought it was a chicken grew old. One day it looked up into the sky and far above it saw a phenomenal bird gliding upon invisible currents of wind. It was utterly captivated and enthralled. "What's that?" the old eagle asked its hen companion. "That," replied the hen, "is the eagle, the king of all birds. He is the bird of birds, the bird of the heavens. But we chickens are mere birds of the earth, and always will be." Soon afterward the old eagle died, still convinced it was only a chicken.

The eagle lived within a constricted horizon all its life, reducing its existence to farmyard mediocrity. It never fulfilled even a fraction of its potential; it never even dawned on this noble bird what it could be. It never became its true self. It was so much better than it ever realized.

How do you find the true self? And how do you become free of the false self? We have acquired this wisdom from the great spiritual master Ignatius of Loyola. Ignatius arrived at this wisdom from his experience of daydreaming in a Spanish sickbed. At the beginning of 1521, Ignatius was a swashbuckling soldier who dreamed of glory, power, and marriage to a noblewoman. But in May, Ignatius was hit by a cannonball that shattered his knee—and his dreams. After repeated and painful operations on his leg, Ignatius was compelled to rest his leg for nine months in order to recuperate. During these long months he lay in bed. He asked for some books on chivalry and romance to pass the time. But instead he was given a few lives of Jesus and the saints.

When he started reading these books, a struggle developed between two selves inside him. On the one hand, something in him was deeply attracted by the figure of Jesus and by the saints, by a life led without care for power or possessions, without worry about the opinions of others. On the other hand, there was another self inside, and it was not about to be banished. This self could not stop dreaming of becoming a great knight, and Ignatius pictured himself again and again as a knight in shining armor coming to the rescue of comely damsels in distress.

It dawned on Ignatius that these different kinds of daydreams left him in two quite distinct states of mind. Although he found himself enthralled when dreaming of chivalrous deeds or a noble career, the enjoyment did not last long. Once he had stopped toying with these possibilities, he felt empty inside. But when he imagined the life of Jesus and the saints, Ignatius experienced a joy that lasted. He began to realize that the desires that left him with an abiding sense of joy were also the desires that led him toward God, while the desires that left him empty after the initial thrill were leading him in the other direction.

Like Ignatius, each of us has two selves inside. For example, a superficial self might identify itself with a glittering career, like today's successful businessman who spends his working life proudly introducing himself as the CEO of a Fortune 500 company. But the businessman then feels utterly lost after retirement, when the crutch of his false self is no longer there to fall back upon. A surface self is all about *having* things (in Ignatius's case, money and a "trophy" wife from the nobility) and *doing* things (as a successful courtier and knight); the surface self is also all about gaining the high opinion of others (being looked up to and admired). Your false self is not a happy self since it is continually under threat: at any moment you could lose your wealth, career, and admirers. There are competitors all around you, ready to rush in and take your place. This false self is also a lonely self. It is enveloped in masks and facades, and puts on "a face to meet the faces that you meet" (T. S. Eliot, "The Love

Song of J. Alfred Prufrock"), keeping others at a distance for fear they will discover how insecure and needy you really are.

When you successfully connect with your true self, you give up this frenetic chase to become the next pop star or billionaire. Your sense of identity is no longer built upon the expectations of others. You know in your heart that you are loved by God, not because of what you have achieved, but simply because you are you. You feel cherished because of a beauty that is more than skin deep, because of a lovableness you used to fear you never had, but that you always did. You let God live in you and through you. You attune yourself to the music of the universe.

How do you recognize which self is at work? *You recognize the roots by the fruits.* The false self does not offer lasting satisfaction. After providing a short-lived thrill, it leaves you with a lingering sense of dissatisfaction, a feeling of emptiness. The true self gives you a joy that lasts, a feeling of serenity, and a sense of at-oneness with yourself and the universe.

There is a continual struggle between these selves. Everyone experiences this: a flow of moods and a spectrum of feelings and desires, from the generous to the self-absorbed. Generous impulses invite you toward the fullness of life, while self-absorbed impulses pull you into self-defeating habits. The true self is attracted by a free way of living; the false self gets bogged down in destructive ways of responding.

MAKING BIG DECISIONS

If you want to live according to your true self, a key principle is this: *never make a big decision when you're down.* If you're down, everything looks bleaker than it really is. You are like the guy wearing sunglasses who thinks the sun is not shining. In fact, if he takes off his shades, he will see how bright it really is. If you make a decision when everything around you looks dark, it could easily be the wrong decision.

One Friday morning, a Jesuit priest gave his students a class on decision making. He underlined the importance of their not making big decisions when they were down. He explained that most people hate being down, so they feel compelled to do something to lift their spirits. They figure that, by making a big decision, they will get themselves out of the morass; in reality, they often get into a worse mess as a result.

On Monday morning as the priest sat working at his desk, a student came rushing into the office. Her name was Susan. "Father, what you said is so true—you're right, they really work." She was so excited that the words came tumbling out. "Hold on a minute," he said. "What are you talking about? What works?" Susan replied, "Your rules about making decisions." He was still in the dark and asked, "What do you mean?"

"You remember you told us on Friday not to make any life-changing decisions when we're down?" she asked me. "Well, I went back to my dorm after class, and my roommate was packing her things. Not just her books or a few clothes, but everything. And only half-way through the semester! I asked her what was going on. She said she just couldn't take it anymore. She was quitting the university. I was stupefied. I mean, this girl has everything going for her. She's charming, bright, good at sports—the full package. It just didn't make any sense, so I asked her why.

"She looked at me and said, 'Being a doctor has always been my dream, from when I was knee-high. Well, it's not going to happen now. I just got the results of my organic chemistry test, and I failed—I mean, I *really* failed. I'm never going to be a doctor now. And as I'm walking back across the quad, like, totally devastated, suddenly there's my boyfriend standing right in front of me. He's with a group of friends, *my* friends, and he turns to me and says,

"Maybe we should call things off for a while. You see I met this girl last night..." And that was it. That was the end. In the space of thirty minutes, my career went down the tubes and my boyfriend left me. There's no point staying any more. I'm off."

Susan immediately remembered the rules for decision making and said, "Please don't go, not now. Don't make a decision when you're down." Her roommate was taken aback. "What's all this about?" she asked. "What do you mean?" So Susan said, "Look, just go down to the lake for the weekend, hang out on the shore, relax, get away from things. When you come back on Monday, you can make your decision then. If you still want to drop out of college on Monday, go ahead. But don't do it now. Not at this moment. You've got to promise me. Okay?"

Her roommate agreed.

On Sunday evening, the roommate returned from the lake. Susan was waiting for her. The girl said, "That was a great suggestion to take the weekend off. You know, I realized that I never really wanted to be a doctor in the first place. It was my parents who pushed it. They pushed it so much that I thought I wanted it too. But I didn't. What I really love is English literature. I've always loved language and novels and stories. That's what I'm going to do. That's going to be my major." Then she paused for a moment and added, "And as for that guy, he was a lousy boyfriend. He was the last guy I needed around me. I'm so glad he's gone." She concluded, "I'm not leaving college after all. I'm staying."

Susan was so delighted that she threw her arms around her then and there.

As Susan finished the story, she said to the Jesuit priest, "Those rules really work. I told her not to make a big decision when she was down. I'm so glad she followed my advice. She would have ruined her life if she had left college last Friday."

Susan taught her roommate an important lesson. Every day people make big decisions out of the wrong psychic space. They walk into marriages and out of them because they feel down. They make friends because of a gnawing restlessness inside. They decide to end friendships while they are full of anxiety and in an upset state of mind.

EXERCISE: PRAYERFULLY REFLECTING ON THE DAY

This is an exercise in self-awareness, done in the evening, and during which you recall the experiences of the day. The objective is not to relive the day, so do not try to experience everything again in your imagination, as though it were happening here before you right now. Neither is the objective to remember every single event as accurately as possible. The purpose instead is to understand the day from God's perspective, in a graced way.

Begin this exercise by asking God for light to illuminate the inner meaning of the events of your day. You will need God's light, because each day is filled with numerous experiences, many so apparently trivial and ordinary that they are easily forgotten. As well as external events, there are also inner reactions, fragments of memory, moments of distraction, and frequent stretches of time where you draw a blank when it comes to recall.

Next, look back over the day in a spirit of thanksgiving, not in a spirit of judgment. There is a big difference between gratitude and judgment. Gratitude comes from the heart and expresses the heart. Judgment comes from the mind. Gratitude sees what is good and beautiful, but judgment often looks for what is deficient, ugly, or missing; it regularly finds fault. If you judge yourself negatively, you will see the worst in yourself. If you are grateful for yourself and your life, you will see the best.

Gratitude unites you with God and with others because it manifests your oneness with the universe, the harmony between you and others. But judgment divides you from yourself and from others, because when you judge, you analyze, dissect, and break things apart. You often judge yourself because you are upset that you are not perfect and you want to be perfect. In fact, nobody is perfect, but that is okay. Be grateful for who you are now: a work in progress, on the way toward perfection but not there yet. Gratitude brings you out of yourself, because you admire people and things beyond yourself, and you give thanks for what there is in the world. But judgment keeps your focus on yourself, on what *you* think and what *you* praise or condemn. With judgment, you get distracted and enamored by your own intelligence, by the complexity of your own mind. With thanksgiving, you admire the good of others and you identify with them.

Looking back at your day in gratitude is like coming down on Christmas morning to open the gifts that have been left in the stocking the night before. What a marvelous moment, full of the joy of wonder and discovery! Compare that to the unenviable task of a sergeant major who inspects the barracks, on the lookout for the least sign of dust and disorder. So as you look back over the day, do it with thanksgiving in your heart, thanking God for the gifts that the day has brought you. Forget the sergeant-major routine!

When you have gone through the first two steps of invoking God's light and recalling the events of the day in a spirit of thanksgiving, move on to the third step, in which you allow the feelings of the day to come to your awareness. Some people find it easy to become aware of their feelings. Women are often more tuned into their feelings, though this is not always the case.

Your feelings are important because they are a clue to what is going on inside. No wonder we often ask each other, "How are you feeling?" We instinctively sense that a person's feelings are an indicator of his or her mood, of how he or she is experiencing life. If your life is difficult, it will be reflected in low-energy feelings such as helplessness, fear, inadequacy, and loneliness. If your life is in bloom, you will feel at ease, optimistic, cheerful, and enthusiastic.

Although feelings are important, you should not identify with them: *you* are not your *feelings*. Feelings are not facts. But don't go to the other extreme either; don't avoid or repress your feelings. Instead, allow yourself to become aware of them. Do not resist this awareness. Your feelings are a language; if you pay close attention to this language, you will discover what your feelings are saying to you.

Now, allow your feelings to surface, whatever they are. Here is a list of several feeling words that may help you: joyous, alive, thankful, relaxed, disinterested, unsure, dissatisfied, resentful, frustrated, powerless. With the help of this list or other words that come to mind, choose the feelings that most accurately characterize the day you have just experienced.

Now, recall that step one was asking God for illumination. Step two was remembering the events of the day with gratitude. Step three was becoming aware of the many different feelings you experienced during the day. Now you are ready for the fourth and most important step.

Focus on one feeling that stands out in a particular way. Which feeling looms largest? Which feeling is most prominent? Which feeling grabs your attention like no other? Whatever you do, don't overpsychologize; don't try to figure out the hidden meaning of this feeling. Remember, this is a prayer exercise, not a therapy session. If the feeling is negative, you may be tempted to condemn yourself. Resist the temptation to punish yourself for having a negative feeling; don't give in to the urge to call yourself weak or stupid or wrong. Simply say to God what comes to your heart as you pay attention to the day's most prominent feeling—your intense admiration and deep gratitude, your sense of being bruised or broken, your need to be soothed and healed, your delight and elation.

Gently finish this review of your day in the loving company of Jesus.

When it comes to reflecting prayerfully on your day, there is always raw material available. The raw material of your prayer is your daily experience—and there is plenty of that! You always have a day of experience right behind you upon which you can reflect. There is much more to this experience than you realize while you are in the midst of it. While you are going through your day, you rarely pause or step back for even a moment. It is only when you come to reflect prayerfully on your day that you unearth the generous presence of God concealed beneath mundane events.

Do you remember the Gospel parable of the treasure hidden in the field? Your experience is like the field, and God's presence is the hidden treasure. At first you only see clay and soil. But when you dig beneath the surface, you uncover unsuspected riches. With the help of God, you find a loving glow that transforms the mundane and illuminates your life in a new way. What was before only ordinary now becomes extraordinary; what was previously humdrum is now sacred. Heaven is constantly brushing against you, and this prayer exercise enables you to find the intersecting point of earth and heaven. God's light brightens up your joy and takes the heavy weight out of your sorrow.

Not only do you always have a day behind you to reflect on, but there are always many feelings connected with that day as well. Some people think they have no feelings because they never talk about them. But not being able to articulate your feelings does not mean you have none. Feelings happen, whether you want them to or not. Even numbness is a feeling. So is detachment. You have emotional sensitivity, and you respond emotionally to experience. In this prayer exercise, you appropriate the day by paying attention to the feelings that have arisen during the previous hours, and then you pray to God out of these feelings.

You should not live your life out of the feelings that surface; simply bring these feelings to God. And do not rely on feelings alone as a guide to behavior. For instance, teenage girls often feel like ugly ducklings. The feeling can be so strong that they unfortunately confuse it with the truth and lose all sense of self-confidence and self-worth. You may be highly intelligent and yet feel stupid, but it would be tragic to live your life wrongly convinced that you had a low IQ, just because you felt stupid. Feeling stupid does not mean being stupid. Feelings are fallible. However, they provide useful feedback. A woman who prayerfully reflects on a particular day, and finds that the feeling of being inadequate and unlovable is uppermost in her consciousness, has received useful feedback that she can bring to God for healing. She has some sort of name for the discomfort she feels. Through describing her pain to God, she can become free of this undermining feeling, and the pain becomes dislodged.

REVIEW

Stories. The first story was the enthralling account of how Ignatius of Loyola, overcome with boredom, started reading the lives of the saints and ended up learning to read the movements of his own heart. The second story was of the college student who was so unsettled by the events of one day that she came close to making a disastrous decision that could have damaged her entire life.

Key phrases. *You recognize the roots by the fruits.* When you are at peace with yourself and in harmony with others, you are most in touch with your core and aligned with your deepest dreams and desires. These fruits of peace and harmony tell you that the roots—your deep-lying hopes and dreams—are in order. At these times you are most yourself, so you can trust the decisions you make. Pay attention to these times of peace and serenity: How do you feel? What is it that guides you into this joyful space? What people help you to be yourself? What activities nurture your true self? Learn from these good times so that you can capitalize on them and always live in harmony with your center and with God. You don't need to take your emotional temperature every hour, but briefly and simply at the end of the day.

Never make a big decision when you're down is the second key phrase. When you feel separated and alienated from yourself, others, and God, you are in the grip of uncertain moods, of feelings that throw you off balance and upset you. These moods and feelings will urge you toward bad decisions. When you feel out of sorts, don't make big decisions! Don't listen to the angst of the surface self. Act against your desolate condition by sharing your pain with others, by seeking advice, by asking friends for support. Ask yourself what led to this sense of dislocation and sadness: Is it connected to the activities you have been engaged in? The friends you have been hanging out with? The movies you have been watching, or the Internet sites you have been visiting? Become aware of what has led you into the darkness so that it does not lead you astray again. Learn to shun it in the future. In the meantime, be patient and do not lose hope: the dark clouds will clear and give way to the sun. There is a light at the end of the tunnel, although when you are feeling so down, you often fear it is the headlight of an oncoming train! Don't rush into any major decisions, because you'll probably be acting out of unhealthy compulsions. Talk to friends, and pray to God for help and healing.

Practical exercise. In this exercise, we invited you to reflect prayerfully on the day. This prayer is based on your felt experience. And where else will you meet God if not in your experience? Experience is the threshold where the divine can enter your humanity. Experience is a great school, though many fail to learn its lessons. But the more you make a connection between God and your emotional experience, the more your life will resonate with the harmony of the universe, so that you will feel the sheer joy of singing your song, the one that God has hummed for you from all eternity.

CHAPTER SIX

Loving Yourself

THE RELUCTANT OAK TREE

Once upon a time, there was a giant oak tree in the middle of a city park. Its branches stretched out generously on every side so that the tree was a welcome haven for lots of creatures. Birds and squirrels nested high up in the forks of the tree. One morning, a small acorn in its hard leathery shell fell from the tree and plopped onto the carpet of grass beneath. It was a pretty little acorn. Luckily the jays and pigeons did not notice it, because had they seen it, they most certainly would have devoured it.

The acorn was happy with life on the lush grass and wanted things to remain just as they were. The last thing it wanted—God forbid!—was to become an oak tree. It had heard frightening stories about oak trees that had been cut down by human beings or had been struck by nasty bolts of lightning. The little acorn settled comfortably on the grass, and in the days and weeks that followed, it sank slowly and snugly into the soil beneath.

Eventually, the water from rain and the warmth of the sun conspired together to transform the acorn into a small green shoot. One day, the shoot cautiously poked up through the grass. It was not happy with this new state of affairs; it had changed and become a new self against its will.

"Well," it resolved, "I'm not growing any taller than this."

However, the park gardener took a liking to this fragile green sprout and started to nurture it. Each day he came by to see how it was doing, and he cleared away weeds so that the rays of the sun could shine directly on it. Before it knew what was happening, the shoot was on its way to becoming a sapling. It was devastated. Not only was life as an acorn irretrievably lost, but now it seemed that life as a shoot was gone forever as well. This really was out of order. It decided that enough was enough: it would not grow any leaves. But the park gardener was nothing if not persistent, and continued to care assiduously for this tender young tree. He fastened it against a stake to help it withstand strong winds, and regularly pruned its branches. In early spring, the first buds appeared, and then the first leaves. The leaves were large and green, and tipped with bristles. On the underside their delicate veins were clearly visible.

The young oak tree decided that this would truly be the end of the road: it did not want any more change. With all its might, it forbade each leaf from changing color in the fall. But the gentle gardener had other plans. He continued to watch over the tree. He watered its roots when the weather was dry. He fertilized the ground beneath it. Over time, its leaves changed to a rich red. Small groups of people began to gather in the park to look at what had now become a giant tree. They gazed spellbound as its leaves blazed red against the evening sky in autumn.

The huge oak tree became a generous home for human beings, animals, and birds. Squirrels built their dens between its sturdy branches. Many kinds of birds, from woodpeckers to red-tailed hawks, made their nests in it. New acorns grew and dropped from the tree to the lush grass beneath. Some were eaten by squirrels and blue jays. Others sank into the soil and began their own long journey to become future oak trees. The tree's dense crown provided a cool umbrella against the sun's glare in summer and the biting wind in winter. Yet the oak tree had still not come to terms with its lot.

But something happened one winter night that led to a groundbreaking change. An icy windstorm descended upon the park and wreaked havoc everywhere, badly damaging the huge oak tree as well. The next morning when the storm had passed, the gardener came by to check on the oak tree and saw that many of its branches were broken. He carefully cut them away and painstakingly applied soothing ointment to the tree. He placed heavy wooden planks around it and encircled the trunk in a wire mesh.

After working a long time on his knees at the base of the tree, the gardener paused for a moment. He turned his face upward. The giant oak tree looked down at his glowing face, a countenance that radiated wisdom and acceptance. At that moment, something changed for the oak tree. It was not a matter of becoming resigned to its fate or tolerating its lot; instead it now recognized its life as a blessing. Its leaves rustled in the wind and even its majestic trunk swayed slightly as it breathed in a newfound serenity and uttered a wholehearted yes.

LOVED AS WE ARE

If you cannot love yourself, how can you expect to love others? You cannot give what you do not have. Picture a large vessel full of water. Now, watch as someone pours the water from the vessel. You will notice that the vessel quickly empties. It runs dry. There is no more water inside. Now, ask yourself, "How can I pour water from an empty vessel?" Plainly it is impossible if there is no water inside. It is the same with human beings. If we spend all our time only giving to others, sooner or later we will ourselves run dry. We will run out of energy. We will lose our zip and zest. For example, if we are workaholics, we will run ourselves into the ground. We need to take a break, go for a vacation. We need to replenish ourselves, recharge our batteries, restock our reserves. We need to love ourselves, to fill our vessels with energizing water.

How can we begin to love ourselves? One way is to realize that God loves us exactly as we are; we do not have to be or do anything else. There is no need to earn God's love, which is such an astonishing thought that many of us find it difficult to believe. Tony de Mello came up with a simple method of illustrating this principle, yet a method with colossal consequences. He used to ask people, "Would you accept that God is at least as good as the best person you know?" This question did not ask too much; it did not ask people to believe in God's infinite or unconditional love. It simply invited them to give God the credit of being at least as good as we are at our best. Most people willingly accepted that God was a reasonably decent being, at least as good as the best human beings.

The implications soon became evident after Tony next told stories of individuals who had messed up their lives, got hurt, and hurt others. He then asked his audience, "Would the best person you know forgive someone in those circumstances?" Most of his hearers nodded in agreement. He then asked, "If God is at least as good as the best person you know, wouldn't God also forgive someone like that?" Only then did the radical nature of this deceptively simple principle become evident. It was truly revolutionary.

Another way of beginning to love ourselves is by adjusting the inner "volume control." First, turn down the volume of the voice of your inner critic. Through the awareness and breathing exercises we have suggested, you will develop the ability to notice self-criticism. You will catch yourself being critical. And that is where the second step comes in: turn *up* the voice of your inner affirmer. When you do something well, make sure you acknowledge the fact: give yourself a pat on the back, verbalize your affirmation, reward yourself with something special.

And still another approach to loving yourself is to "act as if" you are already what you want to be. Think of the kind of person you want to be. Visualize one particular quality you would like to embody in your life: patience, tolerance, respect, compassion, or whatever. Each day become aware of that quality, concentrate on it for a few minutes, see yourself embodying it. Then act out of this awareness and visualization. For instance, if it is courage you would like to embody, each day act as if you were already courageous: fake it until you make it.

EXERCISE I:
LOVING MOMENTS OF YOUR LIFE

Here is an exercise adapted from Tony de Mello, which facilitates greater self-acceptance. What is the idea behind it? Each of us holds in our heart a kind of photo album with love-filled snapshots from the past. The album is made up of memories that have touched and gladdened us in a special way. With the help of our imagination, we can open this album and make present as many of these past memories as possible.

This exercise may not be easy at first, especially if you have never before dipped into your memory bank to recall the good moments of your life. You may have to repeat it a few times before you can profit from it.

There is a wonderful exchange in Lewis Carroll's *Through the Looking Glass*: Alice flatly declares her inability to believe something, and the Queen replies that it comes easily with practice:

> "I can't believe that!" said Alice.
>
> "Can't you?" the Queen said in a pitying tone. "Try again: draw a long breath, and shut your eyes."
>
> Alice laughed. "There's no use trying," she said. "One can't believe impossible things."
>
> "I daresay you haven't had much practice," said the Queen. "When I was your age, I always did it for half-

an-hour a day. Why, sometimes I've believed as many as six impossible things before breakfast."

In this exercise you are not remembering impossible things, but things that really happened. Gradually over time you will be able to recall more and more memories that are hidden deep in the recesses of your mind. Do not simply *recall* these loving experiences; the purpose of this exercise is not simply to remember these events, but to *make them present*, and to *relive* them in *God's presence*.

Before you begin, ensure that you are in a comfortable position. Pay attention to your breathing, and soak in the peace that gentle, deep, and rhythmical breathing brings.

Now return to some moment in the past when you felt deeply cherished, affirmed, and loved. Recall the circumstances surrounding this moment as precisely as you can: Who was involved? Was it a member of your family? A friend? Someone you barely knew? What happened? An act of kindness? Words that encouraged you? A phone call? An e-mail? An unexpected visit? A chance encounter? A smile? An embrace?

Remain with this scene and relive the love you originally felt. Do not stay outside the scene as a spectator or observer. Enter into it. Act out once again the feelings you had then. Be present in the scene as though it were unfolding directly in front of you for the first time. See and feel things in the scene, taste and smell them.

Remain with the scene for a while, continuing to draw nourishment from it. Thank God for this love-filled moment in your life. Then reexperience the scene once more, this time asking yourself where God was present in it. How was God present in the love and joy you felt?

In the West we give importance to reason, and dismiss the imagination as secondary. Imagination is for children, something the rest of us supposedly grow out of when we discard childish behavior. We allow it a limited role in our leisure time when we watch movies, play computer games, and read novels. But we generally see the imagination as an escape from reality, a retreat into the realm of fantasy, a place of unreality, prone to all sorts of distortions and hallucinations.

However, in this exercise you do not use your imagination to escape from reality; you use it to enter reality in a deeper way. Your imagination in this instance is based on the reality of a loving experience from the past. And you use your imagination to intensify the reality of that experience by reliving it.

WHEN LOVE DOES NOT GET THROUGH

Ray was every father's dream son. The eldest in the family, he was a college basketball star and excelled at everything he attempted. His high school graduation was almost embarrassing, because he had walked away with every academic and athletic award. Not only that, he was the most genuine and unassuming student in the school. In his leisure time, he tutored mentally challenged younger students.

He was consistently at the top of his class at college. Nobody was surprised—that was just Ray. It was expected. He simply was outstanding. That's why his parents couldn't believe it when the hospital phoned. Ray had slit his wrists on a basketball court and was found unconscious after bleeding for fifteen minutes.

When they arrived at hospital, they were shocked to meet a young man full of anger. They could hardly believe it was their son. He had lashed out at the doctors and medical staff who tried to help him. It was only after days of gentle questioning that he finally related the truth to his bewildered parents. Ray believed he was only worthwhile because he was a success; because he pleased his parents by excelling; because his college profited by his skill at basketball; because his friends could always rely on him for anything. Inside, he felt hollow. He was convinced he would wind up alone if he couldn't keep up this performance. People would see right through him. He was terrified of failure and believed himself a fraud. The only value he placed on himself was his external achievement, which he couldn't relate to himself. He didn't want to be only a performer. His whole life had been a role, and he believed that was all he was worth. He felt he could never accept himself without achievements to define him.

His unwitting parents, who genuinely loved him, believed they had loved him wholeheartedly. They believed they were showing him love by displaying such pride in his accomplishments. They had no idea that they were putting huge pressure on him. He felt he had to live up to someone he was not at all. "That great person just isn't me," he reflected. Ray felt his life was worthless without the accolades. Although his parents really loved him, the message never got through. It did not take long for Ray's physical health to return, but it took an awful long time for him to trust that his parents loved him.

EXERCISE 2:
BEING HEALED OF LOW SELF-ESTEEM

In the following prayer exercise, use your imagination in order to enter into contact with God. Do this by placing yourself in a scene from the life of Jesus, reliving it as though you were actually participating in it. This form of prayer has been used for centuries by mystics. For instance, we owe Christmas cribs to Francis of Assisi, who encouraged people to re-create Jesus' birth with the help of their imaginations.

If you do not find this imaginative form of prayer useful, do not worry. The point is not to force yourself into a way of prayer, but to find a method that helps you. If this method does not work for you, do not feel you have to use it. You will be in good company. Even the great Saint Teresa of Avila admitted to having great difficulties picturing Jesus in her mind. So there is nothing wrong with you if you do not find this form of prayer effective. Although this way of prayer is often difficult for logically minded people and for intellectuals, it can also be difficult for those of us who have been fed a steady diet of TV, movies, and computer games: we often find it difficult to imagine anything without outside help.

However, you may find this method of praying easier if you link it with your everyday experience of listening to stories. A good story-teller can make you practically see and hear the characters in the story. These figures become so alive for you that a funny incident has you doubled over with laughter and a poignant moment brings a lump to your throat. In this imaginative method of prayer (called Ignatian contemplation), the story of the Gospel becomes just as vivid and alive for you as if a good storyteller recounted it—except this time, you are telling the story to yourself with the help of your imagination. As told by Tony de Mello in his book *Sadhana*, look with your inner eye at the characters in a Gospel scene. Look at them and listen to what they say. As a result, you will find yourself being touched in a deep way. This method of prayer is effective by being richly *affective*: it engages your heart; it deepens your intimacy with Jesus.

Make sure you are in a comfortable position. Center yourself for a few minutes with the help of one of the breathing exercises from chapter 2. First read this Gospel story slowly and prayerfully:

After this there was a Jewish feast, and Jesus went up to Jerusalem. Now in the city by the Sheep Gate there is a pool called Bethesda in Aramaic; it has five covered walkways. In these lay a huge number of sick, blind, lame, and crippled people, waiting for the movement of the water. For an angel of the Lord went down at certain times and stirred up the water; and whoever stepped in first after the water swelled was healed from whatever disease afflicted him. A man was there who had been sick for thirty-eight years. When Jesus saw him lying there, and

knew he had been ill for such a long time, he said: "Do you want to
be healed?" The sick man answered him: "Sir, I have no one to put me
into the pool when the water swells. I'm always stuck here, and before
I can even think of being moved, someone else has stepped into the
water before me." Jesus said to him: "Rise, take up your mat, and
walk." And immediately the man was made well, and took up his mat,
and walked. (John 5:1–9; our translation)

Now put down the text and picture the place in your imagination. Watch the people streaming toward the Temple for the feast.
How big is the Temple? What does it look like? Don't feel that you
have to picture the Temple as it actually was. The purpose of this
prayer is not to have a historically accurate picture of things as they
were 2,000 years ago. The goal is to let God speak to you through
your imagination today. So the people in the scene do not have to be
dressed in the traditional garb of the time, and you do not have to
make them speak the local language. Let your imagination run free:
if the people who enter the Temple are dressed in jeans, do not get
upset. If the street vendors are selling hot dogs, let it happen that
way. If you get fixated on historical accuracy, you will never get down
to the business of praying, because the picture in your imagination
will never be perfect enough to satisfy you. So do not burden your
imagination with the weight of historical exactness: leave it free so
that God can speak to you through it.

How are the people who go toward the Temple dressed on this
feast day? Have they put on their best clothes? Are there destitute
people begging for alms? What is the weather like? Is it hot? What
do the porches next to the gate of the Temple walls look like? Listen
as someone passing by refers to the gate as "the Sheep Gate."

Now look at the pool called Bethesda. How large is it? Look
at the surface of the water. Does the sunlight reflect upon it? Now
look at the crowd of sick people gathered round the pool. Are there

many? What do they look like? What sicknesses do they suffer from? Do they speak? Are they silent?

Do not look on this scene as an outsider, but place yourself inside it. Where are you? What are you doing? Why are you here? What do you feel as you look around you?

Look at the sick people as they wait for the water to move. What happens when the water stirs up, swells and rises? Is it like a sudden large wave that swells up to the side of the pool? How soon do people notice the motion in the pool? Is there jostling as people try to get to the water? Do people argue and quarrel with each other? Do the stronger push the weaker aside as they rush to get into the water?

Now look at the sick man that Jesus goes to speak to. Where is he lying? Is he sad? Is he weeping? Has the man any family? Or are they all dead? He has been coming here every day for thirty-eight years. Who brings him here? Does the man feel he is a burden on that person? What does Jesus say to the man when he draws near? What does the man reply?

Now listen to Jesus' question: "Do you want to be healed?" Let that question sink in. Then listen to the man's response: "Sir, I have no one to put me into the pool when the water swells. I'm always stuck here, and before I can even think of being moved, someone else has stepped into the water before me." Why does the man not stay near the edge of the pool? Is it because he fears being trampled by those who want to get into the water? Does he perhaps now ask Jesus to place him near the water, or to help him get in when the next wave swells up?

Now listen to Jesus' command to the man: "Rise, take up your mat, and walk." How does the man react? Look at him as he stands up on his own feet after thirty-eight years of being unable to stand. Look at him take his first step. Look at the expression on the man's face. What do you see in Jesus' face? What do you feel yourself as you watch?

Now Jesus turns to you. What does he say to you? Is there anything you want to be healed of? Tell Jesus about the sickness of not loving yourself enough. Now listen as Jesus asks you: "Do you want to be healed?" Stay with that question for a few moments. What do you reply? Do you really believe that Jesus can help you? Do you trust Jesus to cure you? Listen to Jesus as he says the words of healing. What impact do these words have on you? Do you believe in their power? Do you believe that Jesus' healing power is working within you right now? Do you believe that Jesus will build up your sense of self-worth—even if you do not see any visible signs at the moment?

Spend a few minutes talking to Jesus.

As you finish, quietly recall the journey you have gone through in this prayer exercise. Do you feel any different from when you started? Whatever you may feel or may not feel, believe that good will come to you as a result of this period of prayer. Slowly exit this meditation in a spirit of calm and peace.

Westerners often have problems with this form of praying Gospel scenes because they feel it gives too much freedom to the imagination at the expense of the literal truth of what happened. But at the same time they are perfectly happy to depict Jesus as a blonde, blue-eyed, all-American boy, even though this image is at odds with the Middle Eastern features he probably actually had. Every culture tends to portray Jesus as one of their own. Most artists depict Jesus with similar features to their target audience. Yet despite the variety of images of Jesus—whether he is depicted as a white European or a black African—people can still be deeply moved by these highly diverse portraits. Obviously, people agree that it matters what Jesus really looked like. Yet concretely, it is often more important for people to see Jesus in a way that is familiar to them instead of trying to come up with a forensic reconstruction of a first-century Jewish face. The lack of history need not obscure the mystery.

It is the same with the imagination. It gives us a means of relating to Jesus in a deep and personal way, even if it does not match the findings of historians about how first-century Jews looked. Many people have been taught that imagination has no place in faith, so they are reluctant to try out this kind of prayer. But once they use it, a whole new personal relationship to God can open up.

Those who hold the Bible in great awe can be shocked at the way this imaginative prayer uses scripture in such an apparently loose and liberal way. They feel that this kind of prayer gets priorities completely wrong, by placing merely human imagination above the revealed Word of God. But in fact the purpose of this form of prayer is not to minimize or distort the Word of God but to maximize it by bringing home the message it holds for us today. What does the Christ of the Gospels want to say to me now?

REVIEW

Stories. Read again the two stories from this chapter. The first tells of the acorn that did not want to become an oak tree. The second is the harrowing truth behind the winning face of the all-American boy called Ray.

Key phrase. The key phrase in this chapter is this: *If you cannot love yourself, how can you expect to love others?* The two greatest commandments in Christianity invite us to love God with our whole being and to love our neighbor as ourselves. Many of us forget the final words of that second commandment: "as ourselves." You are not to love others in a lesser way than yourself or a greater way than yourself, but *as* yourself.

What makes you so lovable? You are a mirror that reflects God: you are an echo that repeats the voice of God. When you love and accept yourself, you love and accept the utter Goodness that created you. When you reject yourself, you are denying the Love that formed you. You are an immortal diamond, a priceless gem destined to last forever. There will be no term or end to your life. You come from God, you are in God's image, and your destiny is God.

You intuitively sense that there is something beyond the flickering images of TV screens, something above the neon highways of the Internet, something much deeper than the hollow promises of consumerism. You need to go beneath the conscious level to find the sweet spot. At times you mistake empty conversations for joy, and you fear you are falling into superficiality yourself. However, you resist outside pressure to be just one of the crowd. You steadfastly refuse to buy into the opinions of others. Instead, you listen to the inner voice that tells you how special you are. You want to be real, and not have to play a role or wear a mask. You manifest your self-worth by how you treat yourself and others.

There is something divine in you. You are a child of God. Because you are a child of God, you are like God. Respect the greatness God has given you. Be receptive to the potential within you. Attract God into your life by esteeming and respecting yourself. Do not look at yourself with contempt. Do not break your connection with God by failing to love yourself. Do not reject yourself, the summit of God's creation, the apple of God's eye.

Ease up on yourself. Resolve to love yourself. Nourish the living gem inside with trust, peace, love, and truth. Only your failure to love can wound this inner beauty. Love yourself, and love others.

Practical exercises. Our two practical exercises in this chapter were reliving the loving moments of your life, and contemplating Jesus' healing of the paralytic in order to build up your sense of self-worth. When you get in touch with the love-filled moments of your past, you will open up your heart to life. You will bring your heart into the light, you will unwrap it, and you will make it vulnerable. And that is how you will rescue it from death, darkness, and suffocation: joy will be your salvation.

If the imaginative method of entering Gospel scenes is for you, you will know it. If it does not work for you, don't work at it. Leave it aside and try another approach.

In this chapter, we have looked at self-love and self-worth. It is vital to trust your own goodness, a goodness that the ups and downs of life often eclipse. And once the clouds of self-doubt disperse, you will be able to see the bright sun of God's goodness. When you can shine the light on your own goodness, you can awaken more easily to the light of God.

CHAPTER SEVEN

Overcoming Fear

HOW WE DIMINISH FEAR

There is a story told in certain African cultures about a huge dragon that terrorizes the tribe of a little village. Everyone is frightened of challenging it; everyone, that is, except for a naive little boy who dreams of being a hero. Inside, he is afraid like everyone else. He cannot remove the fear he feels, but he is determined it will not hold him back. He sets out for the top of the mountain where the dragon has its lair, whistling a merry tune to give himself courage, and dreaming of slaying this enormous reptilian creature.

He has barely arrived at the foothills when the ground begins to heave and rumble as though the earth itself were about to split open. A dragon as large as ten elephants appears, its long green tail flailing behind it and clouds of smoke curling down from its ugly swollen nostrils.

"I heard an abominable whistling sound," it shrieks, "and there is nothing I detest more than music." Then, with one blast of its breath, the dragon hurls an enormous flame in the direction of the boy, immediately burning the tops off all the pine trees in the vicinity.

The boy runs for cover behind the remains of a tree, and stays motionless until the rumbling sound of the dragon eventually fades in the distance. By now it is evening. The boy is still too terrified to move. He spends half the night shivering before he falls asleep against the trunk of the burnt-out old tree. The next morning he considers giving up the quest, but after much deliberation he decides, with the brashness of youth, that he will give it one last try. Moving as quietly as possible, and keeping out of sight, he slowly makes his way up the mountain by the other side, where he knows he will be well hidden by the dense cover of lush foliage and trees.

When he is half-way up the mountain, the boy arrives at an area with loose rock. Though he treads over it as gingerly as he can, a large rock becomes dislodged and tumbles down the mountain. The sound echoes into the valley below. Suddenly the boy hears the rumbling sound of the dragon approach, but this time to his surprise, the earth does not shake as much. He hides behind a spiky green pine tree.

The dragon shouts in its harsh voice, "Who's there?"

The boy clings to the trunk of the tree, and breathes as quietly as he can, his heart thumping furiously in his breast. After what seems like an eternity, he slowly peeks around the tree. The dragon has just turned around and is going back up the mountain. The boy is shocked to see that the dragon is no longer the size of ten elephants, but of only two. What has happened? He is thoroughly perplexed.

When the coast is clear, the boy resumes his patient ascent, all the while trying to figure out how the dragon could have grown so small so quickly. At dawn the next morning the boy has almost reached the top. As he walks quietly along a narrow ridge, he catches sight of what looks like a dragon, washing itself in a pool just four hundred yards away. The boy can hardly believe his eyes: it is only the size of a pony, too puny to split the earth open with a whip of its tail, too weak to hurl trees into the sky like missiles. But taking nothing for granted, he waits until the supposed dragon has finished washing itself before proceeding farther.

Under cover of the shadows cast by the tall pine trees, the boy sneaks furtively along the path that leads to the dragon's lair, his dagger in hand, ready to slay the creature. But when he arrives at the den, he discovers to his surprise that the dragon has shrunk into a tiny lizard, just three inches long. The boy laughs, almost in disbelief, and calmly returns his dagger to his sheath. He looks at the little lizard with a newfound compassion and asks, "What is your name?"

The lizard replies, "My name is Fear."

This story teaches many useful lessons. Let us draw just two morals from it: first, the importance of facing our fears, and second, the importance of acting despite our fears. There are many innocuous things in our world like that tiny lizard; but because of our own anxiety, we have transformed them into ogres that intimidate and subdue us. It is so easy to be felled by our fears. The problem is that we misunderstand them: we think we are confronting a dragon when we are really only facing a lizard. And it is not enough to name a fear for what it is; it is not sufficient to call a lizard by name. A name may tell you a lot, but sometimes a name does not really help you understand your fear, and understanding is vital if you want to be rid of it. The best way to dispel a particular fear is to bring it from the darkness into the light, by sharing it with God and confiding in a friend.

No matter how hopeless things initially appear, they can always change for the better. If you are courageous, you will overcome the obstacles before you and succeed. The dragons you face in life appear under many different guises: from economic woes to health issues to global terrorism. But many of the terrible things we fear never transpire. As Michel de Montaigne once put it: "My life has been full of terrible misfortunes, most of which never happened."

"Courage is fear that has said its prayers" (Dorothy Bernard). *Courageous people act in spite of their fear.* They could easily be cowards, except for the fact that they won't let fear keep them down. They act on their convictions even when they feel afraid. Fear will not force them off course; they unflinchingly pursue their goal.

The little boy in our story was utterly afraid, but he persisted in hunting the dragon anyway. He was not silly enough to pretend he had no fears; instead, he mastered them. He was convinced there was something more important than fear: not just the dream of heroism, but also the desire to help the fellow members of his tribe. All the while, he was not sure whether things would turn out for the best, but had he waited for certainty before acting, he never would have climbed the mountain in the first place. There is something thoroughly noble and admirable in battling for a cause that may not lead to reward, but could jeopardize your future.

The boy hoped for a happy ending to his adventure; we all do. But that does not make it easier to achieve. The important thing is the journey. If fear takes us over, it ruins our life.

EXERCISE 1:
ACHIEVING YOUR HIGHEST GOALS

If you find it difficult to take action because of your fears, try the following exercise. It comprises three steps:

1. Imagine you have no fears about the future—about reaching your goals, about financial security, about your health, or about what other people will think of you. Look into the future, knowing there is no way you can fail.

2. With no fears to hold you back, and with God at your side, next ask yourself, "What ten things do I most want to do in life? What ten ventures would I undertake if I had no fear at all?" Write them on a sheet of paper, from 1 to 10, with number 1 being the easiest goal and number 10 the most difficult. For example, number 1 could be

smiling at new co-workers each day; number 2 could be speaking out every time you feel called to;...number 8 might be living in Tuscany for an extended stay; number 9, returning to college to train for a new career; number 10, becoming the most loving person of this millennium.

3. Here is the most daring step of all: go for what you want, and leave the results to God. Work at making your dream real, starting with the first or easiest goal. It will already be a great success simply by moving toward this goal. Once you have acted and feel comfortable with your progress on the first objective, move on to the next one.

This exercise may be just the practical push you need to get you going, and you will be surprised how far the principle of "acting as if" brings you in the direction of each goal. Take to heart the encouraging words of Ralph Waldo Emerson: "When a resolute young fellow steps up to the great bully, the world, and takes him boldly by the beard, he is often surprised to find it comes off in his hand, and that it was only tied on to scare away the timid adventurers."

EXERCISE 2: DO NOT BE AFRAID

First read this passage (Luke 24:36–43, NIV).

Jesus himself stood among them and said to them, "Peace be with you." They were startled and frightened, thinking they saw a ghost. He said to them, "Why are you troubled, and why do doubts rise in your minds? Look at my hands and my feet. It is I myself! Touch me and see; a ghost does not have flesh and bones, as you see I have." When he had said this, he showed them his hands and feet. And while they still did not believe it because of joy and amazement, he asked them, "Do

you have anything here to eat?" They gave him a piece of broiled fish,
and he took it and ate it in their presence.

Prepare for this period of prayer by doing a brief breathing or
awareness exercise.

First, imagine the overall scene. Picture the room where the
apostles consumed the Passover meal with Jesus before his death.
How big is the room? Is it circular, square, rectangular? Is the ceiling
low or high? Where are the windows? Are the walls just plain or are
they decorated? How big is the table? Is it made of wood?

Now bring the scene itself to life. There are eleven apostles
here. Judas Iscariot, the one who betrayed Jesus, has taken his own
life. The remaining apostles are back in the supper room. They have
been eating fish. Perhaps it is evening. Is it dark outside? Quiet? Are
there candles burning in the room?

Do the apostles talk? What are they saying to each other? Do
they talk about Jesus? About the past? How do they feel? They have
heard that Jesus is risen, but have not yet seen him for themselves.
The Risen Lord has already appeared to some female disciples, and
also to two disciples walking along the road. The apostles used to be
the special ones, but now they seem to be the only ones not to have
seen Jesus. How do they feel about this turn of events? Embarrassed?
Mortified? Do they see it as a just reward for having been so cow-
ardly as to run away when Jesus was arrested?

What is their morale like? Do these men really want to see
Jesus? Or, now that they know he is full of majesty, are they afraid
of encountering him? After all, three fell asleep during Jesus' hour of
agony in the Garden of Gethsemane. One betrayed him and came to
a horrible end. The other, their leader Peter, denied three times that
he even knew his Master. What about Peter? Does he look upset? Are
his eyes red from weeping?

When they hear sudden noises from outside, how do they react? Do they exchange frightened glances?

Now Jesus appears in their midst. What does he look like? Listen to his words: "Peace be with you." Now look at the fear in the eyes of the apostles: they think they see a ghost. The last time they saw him, his hands were tied like those of a criminal, covered with the filth of the world. Do they open their mouths to say anything or stay silent?

Put yourself in this scene. Where are you? What are you doing? How do you react to Jesus' appearance? To his greeting of peace?

Listen to the next words of Jesus: "Why are you troubled, and why do doubts rise in your minds? Look at my hands and my feet. It is I myself! Touch me and see; a ghost does not have flesh and bones, as you see I have."

What is it that Jesus reads in their minds? The struggle between doubt and faith? Between fear and trust? Are their old selves still alive, full of anxiety and suspicion? Have their new selves risen to life yet with Jesus?

What is going on in *your* mind? Can you trust? Do you feel afraid? Can you see the new and risen Jesus? How often do you miss or not recognize Jesus in your daily life? If not, do you want to see and believe in this Risen One?

Watch the apostles' reaction as Jesus tells them he is truly Jesus, the same Jesus, not a ghost, but the One who is risen from the dead, just as he promised. What do they do when Jesus invites them to touch him, when he shows them the wounds on his hands and his feet?

Look at Jesus as he turns to you and tells you he is not a ghost, but real, with a body. What do you feel when he invites you to touch him? Do you dare approach him? If not, does he approach you? Does he lay his hand upon you? What does his hand feel like?

Look at the joy in the apostles' eyes. They are utterly fascinated and yet still uncertain. So Jesus asks for something to eat. Jesus has sat down to eat many times in the past with his apostles. Who brings him the piece of broiled fish? Watch Jesus as he eats the piece of fish.

As you come toward the end of this time of prayer, what do you want to say to Jesus? If you are fearful, focus on Jesus' kindness to you, and it will help you pluck up courage. Speak to Jesus with confidence. He knows what is in your heart. He is still a human being like you, and yet now it is obvious how much more than a human being he is: Jesus is the Lord, the Son of the Most High.

Do you want to be more than just a human being? Do you want to be a child of God? Do you want to cast out fear? Invite Jesus into your heart. Ask him to help you love, for perfect love casts out fear.

REVIEW

Story. Recall the wonderful story of the dragon that wasn't a dragon.

Key phrase. *Courageous people act in spite of their fear.* To act in spite of your fear, you need practice and you need faith. "Do one thing everyday that scares you" (Eleanor Roosevelt).

Practical exercises. There were two practical exercises in this chapter: first, a call to embrace a daring vision through making your top-ten life-goals real; and second, a call to experience the Risen Jesus telling the disciples not to be afraid, and inviting you to take heart.

CHAPTER EIGHT

Releasing the Child Within

A little boy goes to his first wedding. He is enthralled by the spectacle. During the ceremony he turns to his mother and asks, "Mommy, why is the bride wearing white?" His mother replies, "She's in white because she is so happy, and this is the happiest day of her life." The boy thinks for a moment and then asks, "Well, then, why is the groom wearing black?"

CHILDLIKE QUALITIES

Children are not diplomats. They say things that adults would not dream of putting into words. They also have qualities that many adults have lost: innocence, spontaneity, trustfulness, transparency, and openness. They view the world with wonder and awe. Each day is an adventure. They know how to laugh—and how to be joyfully absorbed in the seriousness of play. Jesus says we have to become like little children to enter the kingdom of God. But becoming a child does not mean reverting to irresponsibility. *Become childlike, not childish.* No one wants to imitate the negative qualities we associate with childishness: ignorance, irresponsibility, jealousy, stubbornness, thoughtlessness, and tantrums. However, *childlike* qualities are wonderful.

Mystics have many childlike qualities. They are full of wonder about things so many of us take for granted. Breathing fills them with wonder. They marvel at the fact that this invisible force sustains them every moment. They are also in awe of the beauty of nature. One day, a friend of Tony de Mello's asked him what contemplation was, but he said nothing in response. A few days later, the two of them went down to a lake with a picnic they had prepared. It was evening. They sat in perfect silence watching the light of the full moon playing upon the water. The stillness was so complete that they practically forgot to eat the food they had brought. As they got up to return, Tony turned to his friend and said, "What is contemplation?"

The mystics revel in the tiny things you may be overlooking. The capacity to wonder will give you enthusiasm for little things: you literally will stop to smell the roses. You'll relish a baby's smile, the golden leaves of fall that crunch under your feet, a piping hot cappuccino, your kid sleeping peacefully beside you, a barefoot walk through the grass, a glass of Chardonnay on the deck in summer as you gaze at the clouds as they hang peacefully in the blue sky.

Tony de Mello told the story of a great spiritual master who displayed absolutely no interest in a great healer who lived outside his town. But every day numerous sick people flocked to the healer, looking for cures. And the healer did not disappoint them, because he frequently worked miracles. Whenever anyone asked the master about the healer, they were puzzled by the fact that he said nothing. One day the master was asked straight out why he was so against miracles. He said, "How can I be against what is taking place in front of my eyes each moment of the day?"

If you want help in learning how to live in such a world of marvel and awe, continue to practice the awareness exercises from chapters 1 and 2: experience God through your body, become aware of your breathing, and practice awareness of everything. As an extra stimulus, pick up a book by an author such as Annie Dillard; for instance, *Pilgrim at Tinker Creek* or *An American Childhood*. Fresh and vivid images tumble down the pages—Dillard's gift with words brings the uniqueness and sparkle of everyday experience to life. She once remarked, "You were made and set here to give voice to your own astonishment." Most of us would be delighted to experience life with the same freshness that she does.

Like a child, the mystic is able to enjoy things in a whole-hearted way and then peacefully let them go. He or she does not become attached. The following de Mello story about two monks and a woman concerns nonattachment, but you can also draw the moral of nonjudgment from it. Again, this refusal to judge others is a childlike quality; it is conveyed by those memorable lines from the musical *South Pacific*: "You've got to be taught to be afraid of...people whose skin is a different shade."

Two monks arrive at a river where they encounter a young woman in a long flowing dress. It is a rainy day, there is mud all around, and the water level is high. The woman is understandably afraid of crossing the river on her own. The elder of the two monks promptly lifts her up in his arms and brings her safely to the other side.

Both monks continue on their journey, but the younger monk now has a troubled look on his face. A few miles down the road, he confronts his older brother: "Have you forgotten you're a monk? We are meant to be above things of the flesh. We are not even supposed to touch women. Yet you took that girl in your arms and carried her across the river."

The older monk says, "Yes, I did. And when I got to the other bank of the river, I put her down again. But you are still carrying her" (*The Song of the Bird*, 108).

The young monk's imagination had been working overtime to create a tawdry and offensive episode out of the charitable gesture of his fellow monk. He interpreted the elder monk's generosity in a false and twisted way and then oozed the kind of self-righteousness for which Jesus repeatedly berated the Pharisees. There was no love and compassion in the young monk's judgment, and yet he is the recipient of so much love and mercy from the hands of God. He has not yet come to see the Pharisee in himself, but when he does, it won't be a pretty sight.

Judgment is God's domain, and it is not our place to usurp God's role. God is waiting until the end of the world for Judgment Day. Why should we try to judge now? We get so easily entangled in ego and judgment. Wouldn't it be preferable to make each day a Non-Judgment Day? It is better not to be too severe in our judgments because the angels of God listen to the words of human beings and enter them in the heavenly scrolls. It would not be pleasant to someday hear the words: "Let it be done unto you according to your own judgment."

If you want to practice non-judgment, refrain from labeling and categorizing everything. There is a story about a New Yorker who asks where Boston is, and someone points to a signpost for Boston on the freeway. The man thinks he has found Boston and climbs the signpost. It is large, rectangular, with white print against a green background. He feels the weather resistant sheet of thin aluminum and thinks, "I knew Boston was no big shakes, but this is some letdown! Well, at least I can tell the folks back home I've been there." The man thinks he has found Boston, but all he has discovered is a signpost, or, as the Chinese proverb says, "When the wise man points to the moon, all the fool sees is his finger." Something similar happens when we label people; we get so preoccupied by the label that we don't see the real person underneath. The man thinks he knows what Boston is even though he has never been there. When we label people, we fall into the trap of thinking we know who they are.

Being childlike is an awesome grace, because it means believing in miracles. Children believe in everything from Santa Claus to the Wizard of Oz. They even believe in angels, for they are naturally at home in a world of mystery and marvels. But the complexity of the adult mind easily suffocates the light and so blocks the expansion of faith. While an adult is still debating the wisdom of accepting a new belief, a child with its natural receptivity has in the meantime made immense progress toward the truth, because it lives in a world without limits. The adult has to find a convincing reason; the child simply powers ahead. Christopher Columbus would never have discovered America for the Europeans if he had waited to gather all the evidence before setting sail. He had not lost contact with the child within. Children are so spontaneous that they have a heck of a time trying out new adventures. They don't look for a map before setting out. They don't read the rulebook first. They don't make sure their life insurance is up to date beforehand. The minds of children have not been hijacked by fear of what others think, by worries about their personal safety, or by concerns of family welfare. It is this weight of worldliness that adults have to shed in order to rediscover the lightness of being a child.

Adults have learned to be suspicious of the enormous claims of belief. They prefer to limit their faith to what can be tried and tested. Society tells them to avoid the unknown and to stick to safe answers. Culture teaches them what is possible and what isn't. On the one hand, adults are given enormous freedoms: the freedom to choose to drive hundreds of models of car, or the freedom to eat innumerable types of food. But at the same time, culture quietly curbs the bigger freedoms: the freedom to believe they are worthy of more than a top brand of car or a gourmet meal, the freedom to trust that there are no bounds to what they can achieve. A child still believes that anything is possible, for God is good, and goodness cannot stop giving.

Children believe there is an infinite supply of love in the universe. And so they do not need to master and control their own existence, for they trust their parents. They do not worry about becoming independent, for they are glad to be connected to a source larger than themselves. They do not want to be self-reliant, because they can more than rely on others. They do not count upon their own resources, because their dad and mom will provide. Children have total confidence in their parents—if a child senses danger, it runs to its mother's arms for refuge. This faith is so strong that a child will prefer its mother, however plain, poor, or powerless, to the most beautiful, richest, or most powerful woman in the world. Children radiate an unbounded sense of trust. And they can manage to trust God as well: they easily connect with the all-giving One. They do not need to exist in isolation.

The love of children has no agenda or vested interests. It is uncomplicated—just like their way of telling the truth with delightful candor, which makes them disarmingly straightforward. Children, because of their innocence, are more perfect images of God than the rest of us. *Become like children if you wish to enter God's kingdom.*

CHILDLIKE FAITH

We adults find it much more difficult to believe than children do. A child trusts God's power to do anything. A child's faith is not focused on its own weakness and vulnerability, but on God's supreme strength and resourcefulness. We tend to get undermined by the problems that surface on our side: we get derailed by our doubts, and fail to fix our gaze on God's strength. In the face of the challenges of life and the skepticism of ourselves and those around us, it is hard for us adults to maintain a childlike faith.

There was once a monk who had a reputation far and wide for holiness. Father Francis was deeply spiritual, and was an outstanding preacher and healer. Perhaps for that reason, many monks were jealous of him, and his talents triggered envy in men less gifted and less holy. Once in a vision, Father Francis had been promised by God that he would live to a ripe old age, and God had commanded him to trust this promise unconditionally. So when he became ill with a rare form of cancer at the age of forty, he took this difficult news in his stride, as did his admirers.

His closest disciple was a young man called Peter. With tireless patience and devotion, Father Francis had rescued Peter from a criminal life of violence and drug abuse, and Peter ascended the path of goodness with the same zeal and determination that he had once displayed in the ways of evil. For he still retained the daring that he had shown as a criminal, though now it had become a holy daring, since Peter had broken all ties with his former life.

At first Peter firmly believed that his master would be healed. How could he not? It had been promised in that famous vision. But as the days and weeks wore on, Father Francis's condition steadily deteriorated, and Peter became increasingly distraught. He prayed as hard as he could in an attempt to shake the heavens out of their complacency. But the harder he prayed, the weaker Father Francis became.

Many monks flocked to visit the dying man. Some came from charitable impulses, but others could barely conceal their glee at Father Francis's demise. Peter welcomed the constant stream of guests, thanking them for the honor of their presence. He poured his fellow monks hot drinks and served refreshing slices of fruit. But he refused to let them see Father Francis, who sat forlornly in a quiet and darkened room at the other side of the monastery, his strength gone and his spirit all but vanquished.

Some of Father Francis's most strident critics pressed Peter for permission to see the man whose holiness was legendary. Peter resisted. "Have some thought for a dying man. The sight of you will only bring back painful memories to him," he said.

One of them replied sarcastically, "I would have thought that, with your terrible past, you would be a much more painful memory for the holy man."

Forgetting his own grief for a moment, Peter drew himself up to his full height, looked the monk straight in the eye, and proudly replied, "I am a memory, but not a hurtful one, as you claim. I remind Father Francis of God's Infinite Mercy. And he can die in peace when he sees me, for he knows that he is entrusting his spirit to the same Immense Mercy."

The man smiled, "So he's going to die then, is he?" Peter bit his lip to hold himself back from angry words.

Soon Father Francis was confined to bed. He stopped eating and drinking. The doctor was called. He confirmed what Peter already feared: Father Francis was dying. He drifted in and out of consciousness, and every so often he seemed about to say a word, but no sound left his lips. All that could be heard was a constant rattling from the back of his throat as his breathing became increasingly labored and irregular.

When news of his condition became known, even more of Father Francis's enemies gathered at the monastery. They noticed Peter's despondent look. One asked, "What's the matter? Is it too late? You, Peter, his prize disciple, no longer have faith in a miracle? You're full of doubt, aren't you?"

Peter remained silent, though inside he felt cruelly let down.

Another continued, "God works so many miracles, but none for Father Francis. What do you have to say about that? He has deceived you greatly, your holy Francis. Did he not tell you he would live to be ninety? What has become of the handsome monk now? A feeble frame on a death bed." And the monk chuckled.

Peter turned around and wept silently. He had to face the truth. He had believed, he had hoped all he could, he had consumed himself hoping against hope—but nothing had changed for the better. Sadly he began to walk away.

They shouted after him, "Do you now accept that Father Francis was an impostor? He took advantage of you. He betrayed your trust. Behind your back he sneered at you."

Peter tried to ignore their taunts and walked back the long corridor to the room of the dying man. Father Francis's face had grown deathly pale, and at intervals a tremor convulsed his whole body. The doctor by his bedside gestured to Peter and explained that death could be expected at any moment.

Peter staggered slightly. He stayed a few minutes, slowly whispering the names "Jesus" and "Francis," though both names were breaking his heart. He recalled his own conversion, and the vital role Father Francis played in it. He thought, "And now that I could have really made him proud of me, he is being taken away from me." He tried to pronounce with faith the name "Jesus" again. But all he could say in his heart was, "Why have you done this to us, Lord? Why have you let me down? Why have you let Father Francis down? All our hope was in you!" And he tried to restrain his tears.

When Peter emerged, he found a group of loyal monks had gathered outside. But even they had begun to doubt now. Some shook their heads in disbelief. One or two even cast disapproving glances in Peter's direction.

Peter suddenly found himself on his knees; he knew not what invisible force had put him there. Inside his heart, he heard a voice ask: "Do you believe?" He was so overcome with grief that the words hardly registered until he heard again the question, "Do you believe?" The perfect timbre of the voice resounded through his whole body, as though it sought to instill in him the very faith it asked for. But still Peter hesitated. A third time the voice asked, "Do you believe?" Peter's whole body began to quiver with emotion. He shouted out at the top of his lungs, "Lord, I believe."

At that moment Father Francis became well again.

EXERCISE: THE PRODIGAL SON

Prepare yourself for prayer by means of a short breathing exercise.

The following prayer period is divided into two parts: in the first part. we will help you prayerfully enter into the story of the prodigal son. We will do this by imaginatively filling out the bare details recorded in the Gospel. Read this first part slowly. Pause now and then during your reading to let details sink in. If something touches you in a special way, stay with it for a few moments before moving on. In the second part of this prayer period, we will invite you to have a dialogue with this young man yourself.

Part one. A man had two sons. The older son was obedient and dutiful, and also a somewhat dull fellow. He had little initiative and was happy to fit in with things rather than going to the trouble of making up his own mind. The younger son was much brighter than his brother, but he was lazy, pleasure-seeking, and defiant as well. His father tried to rein him in, but the son rebelled even more as a result.

One day the younger son had a major confrontation with his father. He son said, "I'm sick of your rebukes and my brother's constant grumbling. I want out. Just give me the money due to me and I'll be gone."

His father said, "Think carefully about your decision. You've got so many talents, but at times you're your own worst enemy. You don't like work, you have expensive tastes, and all you want is to have a good time. What's going to happen when you run out of money? Where are you going to turn then? I'll give you your just share now, but if you come back later looking for more, I simply cannot give it to you. That would be unfair to your brother: the rest is due to him."

His son replied, "You needn't worry, I won't be back looking for anything. Just give me my due and I'll be off."

The father called in a local appraiser to assess the total value of his estate and possessions. His land and herds were worth roughly the same as the combined value of his money, ornaments, and jewels. He allotted the real estate to his elder son and the money and valuables to his younger son. As soon as he received his share, the younger son changed all the valuables into money. He went abroad and pretended to everyone that he was a prince. It made him feel more important, and anyway he didn't like admitting that he was "only" a landowner's son. He flung money around like there was no tomorrow: on mistresses, lavish dinners, high fashion, drink, and games.

It was not long before his inheritance began to run out. And just at that moment, the country was hit by a severe famine. All he wanted to do was return home, but he was too proud to go back with his tail between his legs. So he approached one of his former buddies, a wealthy landowner who used to party with him in the good old days.

"Please give me a job," he pleaded.

Although this man had often lived the high life at the young son's expense, he did not feel obliged to return any favors. In fact, he gave him one of the most menial jobs on his whole estate: looking after the herd of pigs. It was foul and smelly work. The young man was so hungry that he even thought of eating what the pigs ate, but for the fact that he would not have been able to chew or digest husks and acorns. He cried bitterly as he thought of how he had passed himself off as royalty a short time before; and even more bitterly as he remembered the good meals back at his family house, where even the servants were treated well by his father.

But he still could not bring himself to return. He felt it would be a clear sign of weakness. He knew it would be an admission that his life was seriously messed up, an open confession that his grand adventure had been one big failure. So he stuck with his miserable existence for a little longer. However, the day arrived when his humility and common sense finally kicked in.

"Why am I so stupid? What am I doing starving here when I could actually have some basic comfort back home? I'll return. But if I go back to my father, what am I going to say to him? I guess I'll just have to tell the truth: 'Father, I have sinned against heaven and against you; I am no longer worthy of being called your son. Treat me as one of your hired servants, but please just give me any kind of roof over my head.' And maybe if I work hard and live decently, he just might find it in his heart to forgive me one day. I know he probably would not believe this, but I still love him. I still do."

The young man returned home, begging along the way to support himself. He wept when he saw his father's estate from the distance: the vineyards were still as big, and there were long rows of olive trees leading up to the house. As he got closer, he was able to make out a figure conversing with some workers in the field. It had to be his father; he had always been on good terms with the men. But his appearance had changed: nothing of the health and virility of a few years ago remained. He had lost weight and grown so much older. His shoulders were stooped; his body was bent down by grief.

The sight of him made the young man stop in his tracks. "It's because of me and my foolishness," he reflected. "I've ruined my father's whole life." The son took fright and was about to turn on his heels when one of the workers shouted to the old man, "Here comes a disheveled beggar looking for money." His father turned around, and though his son was still a long way off, he immediately knew who it was. He moved as quickly as he could down the long avenue, and when he reached his son, he threw his arms around him and kissed him.

The son fell to his knees sobbing. He said: "Father, I have sinned against heaven and against you; I no longer deserve to be called your son. But please allow me to live with the servants. That's enough for me. In fact, it's much more than I deserve. At least that way I can serve you and work for you, and make up just a little for my terrible callousness and indifference. And I know that just to see you each day will be grace for me. It will give me new life. It will melt the hardness inside my heart."

But his father would not hear of it. Turning to his workers, who had gathered to witness the scene, he said: "Give my son a good bath and then get the finest clothes in the house, a pair of brand-new sandals, and a big ring. Put them on him. Kill the best calf we have, and get everything ready for a big feast. Because this son of mine was dead, but now he has come back to life. He was lost, but now he has been found. I want him to become again the innocent child he once was, a boy who knew how to love in a simple, sincere, and unaffected way. My love for him and the celebration we are going to have are really important, because they will help him rediscover this childlike love." The servants did as they were asked.

The older son was working in the fields around the other side of the hill, so he was not even aware that his brother had come home. The first he knew of it was when he returned in the evening and saw how well lit the house was. Then he heard the sound of music and dancing. He called one of the servants and asked, "What's going on?"

The servant replied, "Sir, your brother is back! Your father told us to kill the fattened calf and organize a big celebration because of your brother's safe arrival, and because he is a changed man, as well. Everything is ready to go. We were just waiting for you to arrive."

But the elder son was aghast. "It's not fair" he said to himself. "It's not just because he's younger. It is also because it's like rewarding him for being bad. That's crazy." And he got so worked up that he started to walk away in disgust.

When his father heard, he ran after his elder son and tried to reason with him. "Come on, join us. Don't spoil the whole party. Come on, please!"

But the elder son got even more indignant. "I have always worked hard for you. I have never gone against a single one of your wishes. And I have always been at your side when you needed me. After that scoundrel left, I tried to make up for his betrayal by loving you even more. And what did I ever get in return? Not even an under-nourished goat to have a celebration with my friends! But when he comes back, after spending all your money on a life of debauchery— and let's be clear, he only came back because he was starving to death—you kill the best calf we have. It just doesn't make sense. It's like you're making fun of my loyalty. You're mocking all my honesty and hard work. I cannot believe I've been such a fool all these years."

His father put his arms around his elder son and said: "I've always loved you, and I still love you, more than ever. The reason I've never celebrated your actions is because those actions speak for themselves. Everything you do is a blessing for me. You are a wonderful son, my pride and joy. I can see it clearly, you can too—I know that—and it's more than obvious to everyone else. But your brother needs all the support we can give him. That's the only way he'll get back to being the innocent child he once was. He needs to see that he is becoming a new man, and the world needs to see it as well. I've never organized a big party for you, but that does not mean that for even a moment I take you for granted." The father pointed to his own heart: "You are here, every moment of every day. I give thanks for you always. And as far as I'm concerned, all I have is yours. But it is only right to have this celebration because your brother was spiritually dead and now he has come back to a life of goodness. He was lost to us, and now he has come back to our love."

The older brother relented. He smiled at his father, and they returned to the house arm in arm.

Part two. Imagine that the big party has come to an end and that everyone has retired for the evening. Go to the room of the prodigal son, where the light is still on. Knock on the door. Ask him if you can talk for a while. Invite him to tell you his story. What was it that made him leave home? What was it he was looking for in life? What was it like playing the prince and the big spender in that foreign country? Did he really feel happy in his dissolute way of life? How did life change for him when the famine set in and he ran out of money? What did he learn from the bitter hardship of near starvation? What impelled him to make the big decision to return home? What were his feelings as he made the journey? What did he feel when his father rushed out to meet him? And when his father ordered the party? How was the party? What was it like reuniting with his elder brother?

As you listen to how the prodigal son's story unfolds, remind yourself that his father symbolizes the heavenly Father. If you feel like that younger son, take courage. Trust that, by imitating him and returning to the Father, you will receive an overwhelming welcome. If you identify with the elder son instead, and feel you have been a good and loving child, don't be upset at the Father's joy over the return of the prodigal. Instead, share in the Father's joy and show love for the lost sheep who has returned to the fold.

REVIEW

Stories. There were three main stories in this chapter: the two monks who meet the woman by the river; the monk Peter who finds it difficult to maintain childlike faith, especially in the face of adult skepticism; and the prodigal son who returns after years of debauchery.

Key phrases. *Become childlike, not childish. Become like children if you wish to enter God's kingdom.* Watch how children trust God, and then trust God the way they do. Watch how children love God, and then love God the way they do. When we do something good, we say, "I did that." But a child says, "Lord, for your sake, I didn't pick a quarrel today. I was good. I obeyed. And I am happy because you know

I am good and that gives you joy." Watch how children own up when they do something wrong, and imitate them. If we slip up, we look for someone else to blame. But a child does not look for excuses or point the finger. A child says to God: "I was naughty. And I am sorry because I upset You."

We often complain that we have no role models to imitate. We forget that God has given us children. And children are worth imitating in many ways. When it comes to the spiritual journey, it is not money, power, knowledge, expertise, or hard work that makes us the greatest in God's kingdom. The greatest is the willingness to make one's soul like the soul of a child: straightforward, trusting, self-forgetful, humble, and kind. "Unless you become like little children, you will not enter the kingdom of heaven" (Matt 18:3). Children are great "mentors." They believe in God with a spirit of simplicity, and do what God asks in an unfussy manner. Children are especially sacred because they have God within themselves in a special way.

Practical exercise. We invited you to read the story of the prodigal son slowly and meditatively, and then have an imaginary conversation with this young man about the ups and downs of his life.

CHAPTER NINE

Becoming Who You Are

OWNING UP TO YOUR GREATNESS

A group of eleven-year-old Polish children recently sent a letter to Hans Christian Andersen, the famous Danish writer, to thank him for his fairy tale "The Ugly Duckling." They did not realize the author had died in 1875. The children found his story so full of life that they had to describe what this fairy tale meant to them: "It is you who make us believe that every ugly duckling can finally become a swan."

What is it about the story of the ugly duckling that has captured the imagination of generations of children and even adults? Andersen's story reflects his own life, but it also resonates with every human life. Like the ugly duckling, each one of us internalizes the criticisms of others. We learn to view ourselves as ugly because of how other people teach us to see ourselves. Twelve people may compliment you in the course of a single day, but you will be inclined to give most credence to the thirteenth person, who makes it clear that you are an ugly duckling by aiming a negative remark in your direction. In the fairy tale, the poor duckling does not meet the expectations of the ducks around him. He blames himself for not being who they want him to be. In fact, if he knew himself better, he would not be tempted to hate himself. With greater self-knowledge, he would also realize that he is a being-in-progress, traveling toward a marvelous goal: becoming a beautiful swan.

You are a human being with huge untapped potential. No matter how difficult your present situation is, no matter how weak or incapable you feel, you can be transformed. The trouble is that, when you hate yourself and don't want to be yourself, you actually become fixated on the self you cannot stand. Although there is nothing you loathe more than yourself, at the same time, there is also nothing you think about more. All your psychic energy is consumed by your unhappiness with being yourself. You have no energy or will left for others. And this is what it is like for the ugly duckling.

The ugly duckling has intense moments of loneliness. It is not that there is no one around. In fact, there are many animals and people around, at times too many. The trouble is that they do not like him or accept him. He could happily keep away from all of them and not miss them in the least, so he is not lonely in the sense of being without company. He is lonely in the deepest sense of the word, because he has no friends, no companions, no one who really loves and understands him.

One day the ugly duckling sees some graceful swans with their glorious wings and dazzling white plumage, and he feels a connection with them. He is attracted by their beauty. He feels that he belongs to something greater than the little world he has been confined to for so long. He has a sense of being a greater self than he or others ever suspected. But this is only a fleeting experience, and soon the ugly duckling is caught up in the hard struggle for survival as a long cold winter sets in. You, too, may feel harmony and oneness at certain moments: when you see the dance of a child, when you hear a soprano with the voice of an angel, when you smell the fragrance of a rose, when you are embraced by a loved one, when you eat a juicy green apple after a day of fasting. But this feeling of oneness can quickly become fragmented as you once again get caught up in the distracting rhythm of daily life.

A moment of decision arrives for the ugly duckling once the warm sun of spring replaces the bitter winter cold. He now feels strong and flies to a little stream where he sees three beautiful swans gliding over the still water. This sight reminds him of the last time he saw these wondrous creatures, and reminds him even more profoundly of his own unhappiness. What will he do? He could leave home and win a new world, but he also stands to lose everything. By now though, he is so fed up with his claustrophobic world that even death is preferable. "I shall fly over to these royal birds," he thinks. "Let them hack me to death because I who am so ugly dare to approach them. But it is better to be killed by *them* than to be bitten by other ducks and pecked by the hens."

Something astonishing and unforeseen unfolds. The desperate bird draws near to the sublime swans, bows his head before them, and says, "Kill me." But in the same moment, he sees his own reflection in the water. He is no longer an ugly and ungainly duckling. Now he is a beautiful swan.

In your own times of crisis and decision, you stand to lose a lot, but you can often gain much more by seizing the moment and grasping the opportunity. So why not take a new direction in life? Yogi Berra says, "If you come to a fork in the road, take it." Take a path that until now you have not dared to tread. Isn't that better than plodding the same predictable furrow until the day you die? By venturing into new territory, you will see yourself in a new way. You will see a new and stronger side to yourself, and discover resources you did not even know you had.

The limits of your vision are the limits of your world. The truth is that you are a swan. You need to visualize this truth because you have probably felt like an ugly duckling for too long. You may feel you were born a duckling, and you may be afraid of anything beyond your familiar confines. Like the ugly duckling, you may not dream of the happiness that could be yours. Dare to be what you dream of being. "A vision is not just a picture of what could be; it is an appeal to our better selves, a call to become something more" (Rosabeth Moss Kanter).

THE MIRACLE IS HERE AND NOW

We spoke in chapter 5 of the two selves inside us: the false self and the true self. The ugly duckling is the false self, and the swan is the true self. The false self is easier to hear because it is made up of so many voices. It often starts with the voices of our parents: Mom's voice says things such as, "Mom won't love you unless you behave like a good girl," and Dad's voice makes threats like, "Dad won't be proud of you unless you get onto the football team." Throughout the course of our lives, new voices are constantly added to these first and most formative voices. These new voices bring even more fear into our lives: they tell us what we must do to please others; they make it clear that we are what we possess and what we achieve. These voices are so insistent and strident that they generally drown out the voice of the real self.

Tony de Mello liked to tell a story about thirsty people floating on a raft with nothing to drink. They think they are in the middle of the ocean, but, in fact, they are beside the coast. Because the river flows into the ocean with great force at that point, the fresh water extends a couple of miles out to sea. They have drinkable water all around them. Sadly, they are totally unaware of this. In the same way, you are floating on top of your true self. It is the swan hidden inside the ugly duckling. Why splash around the water like a duckling when you could be a swan?

Unfortunately, we come to identify ourselves so much with the false self that we are terrified of changing. We feel we simply have to hold on to the programming and conditioning we have received, or else we will lose everything. We are afraid of the unknown. Or perhaps it is more true to say that we are afraid of losing the known. There is something "comforting" about knowing I am an ugly duckling. Granted, it does not guarantee a great future, but it does at least offer me the reassurance of knowing I am on the way to becoming a duck. By comparison, the great unknown is seriously intimidating. Yet, at the same time, in our heart of hearts, we know we are made for something more than mediocrity. It would be more than sad if, on the Day of Judgment, God looked at us sadly and said, "You ventured so little."

We are afraid to believe in our own greatness.

De Mello would also recount the tale of the lion that chanced to come upon a flock of sheep. He was staggered to see a fellow lion grazing among them. It was a lion that had been brought up by the sheep ever since he was a young cub. This "sheep-lion" bleated like a sheep and frolicked around exactly as they did. The lion went straight over to him. When the sheep-lion saw him coming, he began to tremble and shudder all over. The lion said, "What are you doing among the sheep?" The sheep-lion thought that the ferocious-looking creature in front of him was thoroughly dumb. Although he was terrified of pointing out what he believed was more than obvious, he stated, "I am a sheep." And the lion said, "Oh, no, you're not. Come with me." So he dragged the petrified sheep-lion to a large pool and said, "Look!" And when the sheep-lion looked at his reflection in the water he let out an almighty roar, and in that moment he was transformed.

Many people are like that sheep-lion. They do not recognize the huge number of untapped talents and gifts they have. When they are asked to do something new, they politely excuse themselves, explaining that it is simply beyond their ability. They are sincere when they say this. but they are also mistaken. Some psychologists claim that we use as little as 3 percent of our potential. Whatever the exact percentage, there is universal consensus that, when it comes to abilities and gifts, most of us are tip-of-the-iceberg people: only a small part of our potential is visible, "above the waterline"; most of our gifts lie hidden and submerged beneath the surface.

It is tempting to become copies of other people, to conform and lose our individuality in the crowd. The comedian Steven Wright tells this joke: "I woke up one day and everything in the apartment had been stolen and replaced with an exact replica. I said to my roommate, 'Can you believe this? Everything in the apartment has been stolen and replaced with an exact replica.' He said, 'Do I know you?'"

Please do not think we are talking nonsense when we encourage you to become who you are. This is not some far-fetched fantasy that has no connection with everyday life. In fact, the magic is *in* everyday life. The magic is not in becoming rich and famous and getting a part on *American Idol*. The magic is in realizing that you are the swan *right now*.

Another de Mello story was about a homeless man who has just spent a difficult day begging on the streets of London. He has barely managed to get enough money for a sandwich and a cup of tea. He arrives at the Embankment on the River Thames. It is raining, so he covers himself as best he can with his threadbare coat. He is on the point of falling asleep when a silver, chauffeur-driven Rolls Royce suddenly pulls up next to him. An attractive young lady steps out of the car and says, "My poor chap, you're not going to spend the night out here on the Embankment, are you?"

And the homeless man replies, "Actually I am."

She says, "I won't hear of it! You're coming to my house, and you're going to get a proper dinner and a good night's sleep." She ushers him into the car. They drive out of London and arrive at a sprawling mansion with its own private grounds. The butler opens the enormous mahogany door, and the lady says, "James, please make sure that this gentleman is put in a comfortable room in the employees' quarters." James brings the homeless man to a modest but elegant room.

The young lady goes to her chambers. She undresses and is about to get into bed when she suddenly remembers her guest. So she slips something on, and walks down the long corridor to his room. She notices that the light is still on. She taps lightly at the door and finds him still awake. She asks, "Is everything to your satisfaction? Was the meal adequate?"

He replies, "*Adequate* isn't the word. I've never had a better meal, my lady."

"Are you warm enough?" she asks.

"Absolutely, my lady, it's the warmest bed I've ever slept in."

Then she says, "Perhaps you could do with a little company. Why don't you move over a little?" And so she comes to the side of the bed. The man moves over and…falls right into the river Thames!

When we're talking of becoming who you are, we are not talking about an illusion. The dream is here, the dream is now. The magic is to be found where you are today. In his well-known poem "The Circus Animals' Desertion," the Irish poet William Butler Yeats talked of the place where all dreaming starts: "the foul rag and bone shop of the heart." Here and now, "in the foul rag and bone shop of the heart," *that* is where the dream can begin! Even if everything smells foul, even if life has become utterly stale, it is still possible to dream a better dream and to make a better life.

Among Tony's many stories was that of the man who was searching everywhere for happiness. He eventually figured that if God would only fulfill his wishes, he would be truly happy. He pestered God with requests and continually asked for divine favors. Eventually God got tired of these incessant demands and promised to grant any three wishes on one condition: that once these wishes were satisfied, the man would never trouble God again.

The man was thrilled. He said, "God, are you really serious? Is it true that I can have any three things I want?"

God replied, "You heard me right. But don't forget: once I grant these three requests, I'm not answering any more pleas. Understood?"

This was the best deal the man had ever been offered. He knew exactly what his first wish was: a new wife. His present wife was a good woman, but he felt he would like a change, some variety, someone new and different. So he immediately handed in request number one. God asked if he was sure. "Absolutely," replied the man.

He arrived home to the sight of distressed neighbors and relatives. They informed him that his wife had just dropped dead of a massive heart attack, and they offered him their sincere condolences. "She was a wonderful woman," they said. "We honestly don't know how you are going to find an angel like that again."

The man nodded politely, though inwardly he breathed a big sigh of relief. "This is worth celebrating," he thought to himself. He poured out drinks for everyone. An hour later, as the drinks flowed, people began to say things they would have never dreamed of uttering when they were sober. His next-door neighbor said, "With all due respect, you're not the easiest man to live with. She was a saint to put up with you." Someone else chimed in, "Not only that, she never once uttered a bad word about you."

The man was upset by these remarks. He did not want to believe them at first, but the more he reflected, the more he saw how right these people were and what a huge mistake he had just made. He had got rid of the one person in the world who knew him for what he was but loved him nevertheless.

He ran to the local church as quickly as he could and said to God, "I'm so sorry. I made a terrible mistake. I'd like to change that first request. Could I please have my wife back again?"

God replied, "Certainly, but remember that's your second request I'm granting now. You've only one left."

Conscious that he had only one wish left, the man decided not to rush things. He turned to his friends for advice. One friend suggested he ask for $100 billion. Another said, "What use would all the money in the world be to you without your health? So why not ask for perfect health and a long life?" But someone else reflected, "Who wants to live a long and healthy life if there is no one to share it with?"

The feedback he received was so confusing and contradictory that, three years later, the man still had not managed to make up his mind. Eventually God said to him: "Why haven't you asked for your third wish?"

The man replied, "Because I'm terrified of asking for something that will be useless." He paused for a moment and then added, "Could you please advise me? What should I ask for?"

God chuckled. "It's about time you came to your senses! Ask that you will be happy with whatever life brings you."

SERENITY

When you are happy with whatever life brings you, you have attained the gift of serenity, and you can be yourself, serenely, your true self. You can arrive at this true self through simple breathing, awareness, and prayer exercises. These enable you to uncover the true self, which is often hidden by the false self. The latter is loud and attention grabbing. It is weighed down with emotional baggage, negative conditioning, and outside distractions. It is pulled in all sorts of different directions by a multitude of voices. They say things like: I'm missing out on life....Who am I supposed to be today?...Don't take any sides in this argument....Am I better or worse than she is?...It will turn out for the worst just when I'm least prepared....There must be something wrong with me if I need help....I can do without people....Always put on a happy face.

A man is sitting down at a high school reunion, twenty years after graduation. He looks around at some of his former classmates, who are now wearing expensive clothes and have arrived at the gathering in chauffeur-driven limousines. He thinks, "Wow, they've really made it!"

That man is suffering from a lack of imagination. What does he mean that "they've really made it"? Some have their names listed in celebrity magazines, others appear on TV, and one is a member of Congress. So what! Is that success? Being a member of Congress has nothing to do with being a success in life. Having wads of money does not amount to true achievement. You set out on the road to success in life the moment that you wake up and realize that this is not what success is all about.

Is having a good job or being famous or being idolized really the key to happiness? Look at the guy with the big job and the even bigger reputation. He is haunted by the knowledge that he never has time for his children, and is in perpetual fear of what the newspapers will publish about him. People can spend years climbing the ladder of success only to discover they are on the wrong ladder. They have wasted their time. They have spent all their energy getting something that is worth nothing. They are afraid. Look at the politician who has sleepless nights worrying whether he will be reelected. Do you call that success? He does not enjoy life. He is anxious, he is tense. Is that a human way to live? And why did it happen? Because he imagined that he was his job, and he identified himself with prestige and power. He was wrong.

Tony relished telling the story of the lawyer who was given a plumber's bill. The lawyer said, "This is outrageous! You're charging me $800 an hour. I don't make that kind of money as a lawyer." The plumber replied, "I didn't make that kind of money when I was a lawyer either!" You could be a plumber or a lawyer or a rock star, but that does not necessarily affect the real you. If you change your profession tomorrow, will you be a different "I"? Are you your job? Are you your money? Are you your clothes?

The real self or the soul is much more focused than the false self could ever be. The real self knows that the true music is in the silent spaces between all the distracting notes. This is because *the soul is connected to a single voice of inner wisdom: the divine voice*. Without the soul you would only be a talking animal, a parrot repeating words it did not understand. It is the soul that gives us our capacity for love, goodness, and selflessness.

The truth is that the task of life is to become yourself in the best sense of the word. It is not a question of selling out who you are; it is not a matter of leaving yourself behind. Instead, it is about coming home to the real you—a journey that brings you comfort and takes away the burden of the false self with its fearful voices that instigate envy, discord, greed, anger, and other toxic passions. In its place is the relief of listening to the focusing voice of love. You never have to be a phony again, and that is a great liberation. The real self is at one with God, and so it shares God's desire for real love. You keep plugged into your real self by loving.

Being a priest or a Catholic or a Christian are not factors that guarantee love or goodness. These factors can certainly help. They offer people structures and guidelines that direct them along the way, but of themselves they do not make people good. The essential factor is the will. When it comes to love, the will is crucial. Love is willing the well-being of the other person and of yourself. We all associate love with a feeling or emotion, since the examples of love that catch our attention most are those involving strong feelings: a young couple falls "madly" in love, a woman is consumed by heartache when her husband dies, a man is feverish with excitement as he awaits the woman who has swept him off his feet. But we also know that feelings can change like the weather, influenced by minor details, such as the amount of sleep we have had, or how well we have digested our food. It would be shortsighted to identify love with a feeling, since feelings are so fickle. But it would also be blind to refuse any place to feelings. Thankfully, love is often carried on the wings of emotion.

We mourn those who die. We weep at their funerals. We get anxious at the thought that we too must one day die. But we do not worry about walking around as living dead in the meantime. The truth is that when we no longer love, we ourselves have become living corpses. We can still laugh and joke—we can even hold down a decent job—but if love has died in our hearts, our souls have become corpses. The greatest love we can exercise toward ourselves and others is to revive a dead soul, one that has died through wrongdoing and evil.

EXERCISE: WRITING YOUR EULOGY

Death is most often unwelcome. We do not want to die. The following exercise is not so much about death itself; rather it is intended to help you discover your dreams. In order to find your dreams, we invite you to write your own eulogy. However, if you are currently grieving a loved one, or have recently undergone a traumatic experience of death, think carefully before trying this exercise. If you find it too challenging to do alone, why not do it together with a friend? This will give you much-needed support.

Here is the exercise: Imagine that you have died. The day has come for your funeral. Now, allow yourself to dream big dreams, and write the eulogy that you would like to hear read at the ceremony. Cover the following points:

- What did you live for? What was important for you in life? What were your values?

- What difference did your life make? What did you accomplish? In what way is the planet different because of the time you spent upon it? What is your legacy?
- What qualities do you want people to identify in your character? What stories do you want people to remember you by?

When you have finished writing your eulogy, return to the present moment. Become aware of the fact that you are still alive, that you still have a future in front of you. Would you like to live that future differently as a result of what emerged through writing your eulogy? Do you see yourself differently now? Most people who do this exercise become aware of the fact that they want to be remembered for making a difference in the world. Even though they are aware of their fears and failures, they want to be aligned with something greater: the love at the heart of the universe. They want to make an impact that will last. The form of this impact will vary enormously. By identifying what concrete impact you want to make, you discover what your dream is.

Now, turn to God and share what this experience of writing your eulogy has meant for you. Finally, ask for help in making your dream come true. Ask God to empower you to become the person you want to be.

REVIEW

Stories. There were many stories in this chapter: the ugly duckling, the thirsty people on the raft, the sheep-lion, the homeless man in London, the man who gets three wishes from God. Which was your favorite story? Why? Does that tell you anything about yourself?

Key phrases. The first key phrase: *The limits of your vision are the limits of your world.* Expand your vision through cultivating a sense of wonder. To wonder, to imagine, means that you don't take the world as it is. You don't relax into the usual certainties. You find time to be astonished and amazed, to be curious, and to call into question. Through the gift of wonder, you come to see the tremendous depth in familiar things. As the English poet Gerard Manley Hopkins wrote, "There lives the dearest freshness deep down things" ("God's Grandeur").

Learn how to see the world in a new way. The English poet Robert Browning treated his invalid wife Elizabeth Barrett Browning with such reverence and affection that she once wrote to one of her sisters: "And now I begin to wonder naturally whether I may not be some sort of real angel after all." It takes great imagination to be constructive instead of critical, to overlook the cracked cement and instead notice the flowers that rise through it.

The second key phrase: *The soul is connected to a single voice of inner wisdom: the divine voice.* Echoing the words of Jesus in the Gospel of Matthew, we say to you: Do not get too worried about your future. We do not know how much future lies ahead of us. Do not worry about what you will eat to nourish yourself. Do not worry about the clothes you will wear. The life of your soul is far more important than your stomach or your appearance. Look at the birds in the sky. They do not sow seeds, they do not reap the harvest, they do not gather into barns—and yet they do not starve because your Heavenly Father feeds them. You are a human being, you are God's favorite creature, you are worth much more than they are (paraphrase of Matt 6:25–33).

However talented or resourceful you are, you cannot add one inch to your height. If you cannot make yourself even one inch taller, how can you possibly change your whole future to become perfectly healthy, incredibly wealthy, and wonderfully long-lived? Can you order death around and say: "Don't come until I give you permission!" Of course not! What is the point of worrying about the future then?

Do not be anxious about what lies ahead. Leave such worries to people who do not have your great certainty of being a child of God. The Father knows your needs and loves you. Trust him! Put your energy into seeking what is really necessary: love, faith, and kindness.

So do not be distracted by the surface self. Do not get upset about things that are not worth the trouble. Do not worry about tomorrow, for tomorrow will take care of itself. You already have today's tasks and yesterday's memories to occupy you. Why add the weight of tomorrow's uncertainties? There is enough hassle in today without searching out future ones to make you even more upset. Let each of your days be God's today.

Practical exercise. We invited you to write your own eulogy.

HOPE

As this book comes to an end, we thank you for setting out upon a wonderful journey. We encourage you to move forward with hope. You will find your source of hope in the felt experience of God's love for you. Continue to cultivate your relationship with God by saying yes to God's overflowing love for you. If you continue to listen and speak to God, you will come to know your true self, and you won't be limited by a narrow vision.

Keep hoping in God's goodness and your own potential: this will give you the belief that you can reach all good things and God as well.

Annotated Bibliography

Not every idea, insight, or suggestion in our book comes from de Mello. In fact, our book is not about de Mello: it is a guide and a map to prayer and to changing one's life. We certainly draw a lot of inspiration from de Mello, but we do not limit ourselves to him. This applies to our stories and citations as well. Moreover, in certain respects, we go beyond him. This will become more evident in the specific remarks we will make here.

First, let us say something about a few of de Mello's books and books about him, and in the process you'll also get a taste of what has excited and interested us in his spirituality.

Sadhana: Christian Exercises in Eastern Form, New York: Doubleday, Image, 1984. Originally published in 1978, this is de Mello's first book and, in many ways, his best. He wrote it reluctantly and under pressure from a nun who was convinced (correctly) that a book of prayer exercises would satisfy a huge hunger in the reading public. The Sanskrit word *sadhana* means "spiritual effort, training, or discipline." The book comprises forty-seven exercises to help people enjoy prayer by acquiring the skill (and grace) of praying with the heart instead of with the head. De Mello did not simply offer prayer exercises; he also reflected upon them afterward with his reader, explaining why he chose them and how they can be of help in nourishing the body and the soul.

The first fourteen exercises focus on awareness, a notion that was central for de Mello. Awareness is about looking, listening, tasting, touching, and smelling in an accepting way. It is about watching reality without judging it. We have adapted some of de Mello's awareness exercises in our book: for instance, our bodily awareness exercise from chapter 1, and our breathing awareness and sound awareness exercises from chapter 2. The second set of eighteen exercises in *Sadhana* uses fantasy, by which de Mello meant the art, not just of remembering something from the past, but reliving it. One of the sources for these fantasy meditations is the spirituality of Saint Ignatius of Loyola. Like de Mello, we have used Ignatius's imaginative model in order to relive scenes from Jesus' life; for instance, in our meditation from chapter 4, "Seeing a Loving God." The final section of the book *Sadhana* consists of fifteen exercises in devotion, which come mainly from the Christian tradition. We use this devotional model in chapter 3 of this book, applying it to the Prayer of Saint Francis of Assisi and to the Our Father. Despite *Sadhana*'s enormous success, de Mello had misgivings about it. He was worried that it would fix a certain image of him in the mind of readers, and not allow him to grow and develop.

The Song of the Bird, New York: Doubleday, Image, 1984. This second book of de Mello's is a distinct shift in approach from *Sadhana*. This book sets the template that de Mello follows for most of his subsequent writings. No longer is de Mello offering methods of prayer; now he simply tells one story after another. De Mello preferred telling stories to providing meditation exercises (as he had done in *Sadhana*) because stories gave him more freedom as an author and as a man. Readers had followed his prayer exercises in *Sadhana* to the letter, but he knew they could not do the same with stories. They could not ascribe a clear, fixed meaning to tales that spoke at so many different levels. Readers could not pin down stories, and by implication they could not pin down de Mello either. He would remain free, and freedom was something he deeply cherished.

De Mello knew from his experience that stories transcend cultural barriers. They have universal appeal. They are also enduring:

they stay in the mind long after rational arguments are forgotten. To ensure that these stories would be remembered and bear fruit, he advised readers to reflect on the stories, carry them around in the mind, let them sink in, and most of all refrain from applying them to others. As he said: "Every one of these stories is about *you*, no one else" (xvi). "The Golden Eagle" (96) is one of our favorites from this collection, and you will find it and others such as "The Monk and the Woman" (108) mentioned here in our book. Many of these stories have a short moral tagged on at the end, an attempt by de Mello to provoke readers into reflecting on these stories and internalizing them.

One Minute Wisdom, New York: Doubleday, Image, 1988. First published in 1985, two years before de Mello's death, *One Minute Wisdom* is designed for a busy world where most people have little time at their disposal. Each story takes at most a minute to read, though much longer to absorb. The author of these anecdotes, simply called "the Master," is a collective name representing the wise sages of every religion and of none. At the beginning, de Mello articulates his hope for prospective readers: "As you read the printed page and struggle with the Master's cryptic language, it is possible that you will unwittingly chance upon the Silent Teaching that lurks within the book, and be Awakened—and transformed." De Mello refrains from commenting on these stories and parables: he leaves this task to the reflective reader. The opening story in our book comes from this collection.

One Minute Nonsense, Chicago: Loyola Press, 1992. The stories in this book feature the same universal Master that figured in *One Minute Wisdom*, a seer who is everyone and no one: Christian monk, Jewish rabbi, Hindu guru, Sufi mystic, and so on. *One Minute Wisdom* and *One Minute Nonsense* are twin volumes. *One Minute Nonsense* is again tailor-made for a culture where we are accustomed to consume things at alarming speed, and just as quickly discard them. Once again, each story can be read in a minute. These brief stories can be dismissed as nonsensical, but that judgment says more about our craziness than anything else. It is only to be expected that someone trying to put what is inexpressible into words will sound mad to our all too reasonable ears.

Awareness: The Perils and Opportunity of Reality, New York: Doubleday, Image, 1997. Although he could write well, Tony de Mello considered himself a speaker of the word. Perhaps we could say of him what Daniel Boorstin said of Socrates: "For him it was the spoken word, the encounter between living people, with the word as the catalyst of thought, that struck sparks. And the spoken word had an enticing elusiveness, not found in writing, which always invited scrutiny" (Daniel Boorstin, *The Seekers*, New York: Vintage, 1999, p. 28). The book *Awareness* tries to "capture" something of de Mello's live talks on paper, even though de Mello himself once commented: "It is only possible to dissect a dead butterfly." The book is a collaborative effort between many individuals who listened to de Mello over the years, and shared their notes. We use several stories from *Awareness* in our book: for instance, the story of the sheep-lion (57), and the tale of the homeless man from London (32–33).

Joseph Pulickal, compiler, and Aurel Brys, editor, *We Heard the Bird Sing: Interacting with Anthony de Mello, S.J.*, Chicago: Loyola Press, 1995. This is a fascinating collection of anecdotes and testimonies about Tony de Mello by friends, students, and disciples. All contributions are anonymous. It gives intriguing glimpses of the man behind the myth. It shows that Tony was just as human as the rest of us. It turns out he was not a plaster guru, a man of unshakable certainty, but someone who suffered from more than his fair share of doubts and fears. For example, in a letter from 1986 he wrote:

> Last night I had a horrible experience—one of the worst experiences of my life—and I could not sleep very much. It would take too long to describe, but it was a kind of

feeling of despair and fright and terrible loneliness…as if nobody could reach me, no one could touch me, I was just abandoned by God and everyone. And I woke up with such a fright, sweating in spite of the intense cold, so I had to open the windows and walk up and down the room. If that despair had lasted longer I felt I would go mad. (112)

Anand Nayak, *Anthony de Mello: His Life and His Spirituality*, Dublin: Columba Press, 2007. Written by an Indian professor of theology and former Jesuit, who was a friend and student of de Mello's, this book offers a short and illuminating biography of de Mello, from which we have greatly benefited. It also outlines his spiritual teachings, and carefully examines the findings of the Vatican notification about de Mello, asking whether de Mello is a menace for the Catholic faith, and concluding that he is "a prophetic and mystical teacher whose works have brought immense help to a vast number of people and continue to do so" (209).

In the body of our book, we wrote about Tony de Mello in highly positive terms. But now let us take a critical distance. We have acquired permission from Tony himself: he was clear that he never wanted to be anyone's guru, and we are prepared to take this desire of his seriously. So please be warned: we are not about to treat him as a guru, and we have no intention of calling ourselves his disciples.

On June 15, 1983, I (Tom) traveled to a rundown, ramshackle retreat center in the middle of the Irish countryside, with a group of more than fifty Jesuits. We had come to hear the great man himself, Tony de Mello. This retreat, which began on June 15 and ended on June 23, was exclusively for Jesuits, an in-house audience of his fellow members of the Society of Jesus. I was twenty years old at the time. I had started out on my life as a seminarian a couple of years before, and was excited to encounter this renowned spiritual master face-to-face for the first time. Tony de Mello spoke to us for five hours each day. Generally, I find it difficult to listen to anyone for more than an hour at a time, but Tony was such a wonderful communicator that I was totally enthralled—he made us laugh and cry and everything in between. He was a free spirit, and invited all of us to taste and live freedom in our own lives. There was real quality and depth to what Tony said. One of the great Irish spiritual teachers of our day, the late John O'Donohue, used to complain of what he called "Big Mac Spirituality." He felt that too many writers were serving people substandard food instead of solid nourishment, spineless ideas rather than words that really say something. There was none of that "mushiness" in de Mello. He had great spiritual riches to share with us. There was something really positive about Tony's willingness to mine for wisdom in all sorts of unexpected places, to cast his spiritual net as wide as possible. We are living in a globalized world, and it makes sense to borrow insights from everywhere. But at the same time, because he had a pick-and-mix spirituality that took something from here and something from there, it was not always clear if there was a core, and, if so, what that center was.

De Mello was a great performer and a born entertainer. I found it best not to accept everything he said at face value. He liked to use extreme language and often exaggerated. I felt that was part of his prophetic role. Much of what he said was tongue in cheek. For those Christians who never encountered him in the flesh, and only discovered him through the written word, some of what he has written can sound alarming. Eleven years after de Mello died, the Vatican's Congregation for the Doctrine of the Faith issued a "spiritual health" warning about de Mello, like what you would see in another context on cigarette packaging. The judgment of the Vatican was based on a close reading of books by de Mello and books attributed to him. Unfortunately, Tony's mischievousness and free spirit can be misunderstood as something more sinister when they appear in written form. This is why he himself preferred the spoken to the written word.

Unlike Tom, I (Peggy) did not have the pleasure of meeting Tony de Mello face to face or following one of his workshops. However, I have listened to him on tape for dozens of hours, watched him on film, and spent many hours talking with Tom about him. I have also read and reflected upon de Mello's writings. I was blown away by his unbelievable charisma, his magic way with words, and his marvelous ability to teach people how to pray. But at the same time, I did not turn into a devotee, because I noticed a distinct lack of responsibility for "the other" in de Mello, and for me this communal dimension of faith is vital. I believe I have a responsibility toward the other: it informs my political views and it is based on my faith. But this is not de Mello's priority. The main instrument presented in de Mello's books is awareness, with almost no emphasis on community. Now, it is true that spiritual growth is an individual process. In *Awareness*, de Mello says: "Do you want to change the world? How about beginning with yourself? How about being transformed yourself first?" (37) However, change also seems to end with the solitary self in de Mello. Perhaps his point is that, once you are changed, you will not have to worry about changing the world. You will either radiate a goodness that will affect others, or else you will be detached, and it simply will not bother you if other people change or not! De Mello does not feel it is important to remind us that we are our brother's keeper. He does not seem to touch on what Matthew 25 tells us are indispensable actions: feeding the hungry, giving drink to the thirsty, clothing the naked, sheltering the stranger, taking care of the sick, and visiting prisoners. As Terry Eagleton puts it in his book *The Meaning of Life*, these actions are actually the key to life's meaning: "Eternity lies not in a grain of sand but in a glass of water. The cosmos revolves on comforting the sick" (164–65). With all respect for de Mello, being aware is simply not enough when it comes to following Christ.

Tony de Mello's spiritual methodology does not work for me. He encourages me to read a story, absorb it, carry it around all day, and see my day and my life through the prism of that story. I find this method too narrow and too inadequate. It is not strong enough to be the basis of my spirituality. It is just one tool in a spiritual toolbox, but it is not the whole box. My whole person would be limited if awareness were my only avenue. I have listened to him recount one story piled upon another, and it is like eating hot fudge sundaes all afternoon—it is simply too rich for a steady diet. I realize we are meant just to dip in for a taste, and not make a whole meal of it, yet the sheer glut of stories is indigestible. I know in his books he tells us to take one story at a time, but in his public talks, they are simply jammed together. There is just too much to absorb.

Now that we have each spoken in our own name, we will return to speaking together, and fill you in on background details of various chapters in our book. At the beginning of chapter 3, we related a brief anecdote about how the Dutch spiritual writer and pastor Henri Nouwen seemed to be distracted and ill at ease whenever he prayed. The reason we told this story was to show that no two people pray in the same way, but also to encourage you: if a famous spiritual author struggled to pray, you should not be too worried if you find it difficult. Nouwen was admirable: although hugely successful as a university chaplain and teacher, he took a "downwardly mobile" move by choosing to live and work in a community for people with intellectual disabilities. At Nouwen's funeral eulogy, Jean Vanier, the founder of the worldwide L'Arche community, uttered these moving words:

> Having known Henri over a number of years, the first thing I want to say is that he was a man of great energy, vision and insight, but also a man of great pain. Anguish

often fuelled many of his activities, his movement. In many ways he was a man of movement. I was always moved when I sensed the depth of his pain. But Henri had discovered something, for even though in some ways he was running away from pain, at the same time he chose to walk through pain; he accepted anguish; he did not build up barriers to protect himself. In a mysterious way he was a wounded healer, the name of one of his first books.

Also in chapter 3, we told Simone Weil's delightful version of an Eskimo story about a blackbird that intensely desired the light. Like de Mello, Weil was wary of any definitions of God. But compared to de Mello, she was a thoroughly tortured soul. In line with Nietzsche's claim that what does not kill us makes us stronger, her spiritual insights were all the more breathtaking because of her inner suffering. De Mello was an impressive man, but Simone Weil was in a league of her own. This Jewish mystic was immeasurably more patient than de Mello: Whereas he loved the instant gratification of adoring audiences and eager disciples, she was ready to wait humbly on God. He spoke of awareness; she fixed her gaze on attention. De Mello's awareness had an anti-intellectual streak: he wanted us out of our heads and into our bodies. Weil was the opposite: she recommended developing attentiveness through the life of study, and described prayer as paying attention to God. In fact, she tells the story of the blackbird seeking light in an article on study, called "Reflections on the Right Use of School Studies with a View to the Love of God" (from the book *Waiting for God*). De Mello would never have dreamed of suggesting study as a way of cultivating love of God. De Mello may appeal to atheists as well as believers, but Weil, for all her eccentricities, identified herself with those who were outside institutional religion, not to mention with factory workers and the starving. Indeed, it was because she insisted on limiting her food to the ration of her French compatriots that she died in England in 1943 at the young age of thirty-four.

At the beginning of chapter 5, we said that the real issue for many people is not first of all God, but themselves: "Who am I?" This insight is not from de Mello. It goes back at least to Socrates, to a long and venerable tradition of self-examination. Where do you start, if not from yourself? How can you start somewhere where you are not? These questions are rhetorical, because it is evident that each of us must start from ourselves. To claim as much is a matter of enlightened common sense. When we asserted in chapter 5 that 95 percent of your problems are spiritual, we were exercising our own prophetic right to exaggerate, indulge in hyperbole, and use poetic license! Obviously, there is no such proven statistic: how would you set about proving this from a scientific or empirical point of view?

Our discussion of the true and false self in chapter 5 was inspired by Thomas Merton's famous discussion of this issue in *New Seeds of Contemplation*. Although we have little else to say about Merton, this is not for lack of respect, but because we would need a whole book to do justice to this spiritual giant. Where does the story from the same chapter about the college student called Susan originate? You recall that her roommate was about to quit everything, but luckily learned not to make a decision when she was down. We first heard this story from a Chicago-based Jesuit, whose name we have forgotten. (In our defense, all we can say is that it is impossible to remember the name of every Jesuit, since when we last counted, there were more than 15,000 worldwide.) If you get to read our book, Susan, we would love to hear from you and find out where you are in your life. The wisdom Susan learned and saw dramatically illustrated through her roommate—never make a decision when you are down—goes back to the founder of the Jesuits, Saint Ignatius of

Loyola, although he used a more "spiritual" phrase to say essentially the same thing.

In chapter 6, we recalled how de Mello used to ask people, "Would you accept that God is at least as good as the best person you know?" This creative and striking question stayed with me (Tom) after the week-long retreat I did with Tony in Ireland in June 1983.

In chapter 8, we told the story of the saintly Father Francis who, despite God's promise that he would live to a ripe old age, contracted a rare and deadly form of cancer at the age of forty. His illness is above all a trial for his young disciple Peter, who must make a huge effort to believe, in the face of opposition from his fellow monks, that God would heal Father Francis. We were inspired to create this story as a response to two other extraordinary stories. One is the account of the death and return to life of Lazarus in the Gospel of John (chapter 11). The other is a story from Dostoevsky's *The Brothers Karamazov*: the tale of the death of the Christ-like monk Father Zosima. To the shock of the monks in his community, Zosima's corpse quickly began to rot once he died, in seeming contradiction to the pure life he had lived. The Gospel story and that of Dostoevsky gave us the raw material from which to shape our own story of faith and resurrection.

Tony de Mello liked to shake people up, and his shaking worked. We have incorporated his insights, and have also gone beyond them. We invite you to undertake your own journey and to go beyond us too. That would be the greatest tribute you could give.

Spiritual Masters for All Seasons
Michael Ford

Invites four spiritual masters onto the same stage
for the first time and shows how they speak—
Thomas Merton, Henri Nouwen, Anthony de Mello, and
John O'Donahue—while assessing their place
in the world of contemporary spirituality.

055-7   Paperback

Walking with Thomas Merton
Discovering His Poetry, Essays, and Journals
Robert Waldron
Foreword by Patrick Hart, OCSO

An appreciation, in journal form,
of Thomas Merton as spiritual
writer, monk, and poet.

4058-6   Paperback

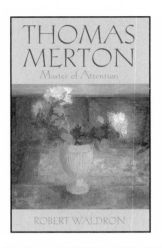

Thomas Merton—
Master of Attention
An Exploration of Prayer
Robert Waldron

Fully explores the inner life of perhaps the best-known
writer on prayer of the twentieth century.

4521-8   Paperback

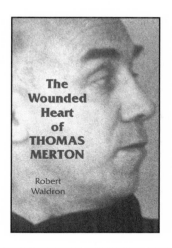

The Wounded Heart of Thomas Merton
Robert Waldron

Examines the life, poetry, letters, and dreams of
Thomas Merton using Jungian archetypes.
The result reveals a monk—and the man within—
and his struggles with "the true self."

4684-0   Paperback

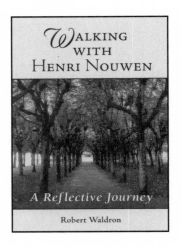

Walking with Henri Nouwen
A Reflective Journey
Robert Waldron

Reflections on Nouwen's life by an experienced teacher and retreat-giver.

4161-2   Paperback

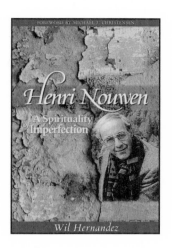

Henri Nouwen
A Spirituality of Imperfection
Wil Hernandez

A synthesis of Nouwen's integrated approach to
spiritual formation which is both driven and tempered
by his embodied spirituality of imperfection—
whereby we learn that the journey to
perfection is through imperfection.

4434-4   Paperback

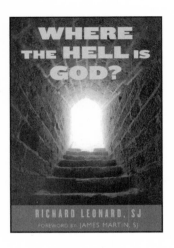

Where the Hell Is God?
Richard Leonard, SJ
Foreword by James Martin, SJ

Combines professional insights along with the author's own experience and insights to speculate on how believers can make sense of their Christian faith when confronted with tragedy and suffering.

060-1   Paperback

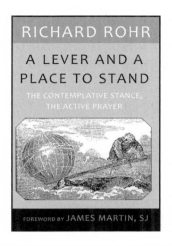

A Lever and a Place to Stand

The Contemplative Stance, the Active Prayer
Richard Rohr
Foreword by James Martin, SJ

Explores the challenges, the rewards, the call, and the possibilities of integrating a sincere inner life with an active life of engagement with the pain of the world.

064-9   Paperback

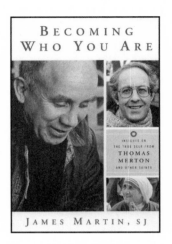

Becoming Who You Are
Insights on the True Self from
Thomas Merton and Other Saints
James Martin, SJ

By meditating on personal examples from the author's
life, as well as reflecting on the inspirational life and
writings of Thomas Merton, stories from the Gospels,
as well as the lives of other holy men and women
(among them, Henri Nouwen, Thérèse of Lisieux and
Pope John XXIII) the reader will see how becoming
who you are, and becoming the person that
God created, is a simple path to happiness,
peace of mind and even sanctity.

036-X   Paperback

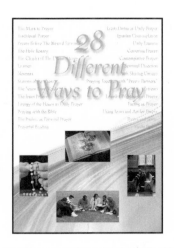

28 Different Ways to Pray

Offers the rich tradition of prayer forms that people
have found helpful in their spiritual lives. The twenty-eight
possible ways to enrich one's prayer life include Centering
Prayer, Liturgy of Hours, Novenas, Stations of the Cross,
Lectio divina, the Jesus Prayer, the Psalms,
the Examen, and many others.

4705-2   Paperback

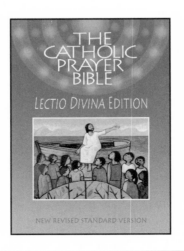

The Catholic Prayer Bible (NRSV)
Lectio Divina Edition
Paulist Press

An ideal Bible for anyone who desires to reflect on the individual stories and chapters of just one, or even all, of the biblical books, while being led to prayer though meditation on that biblical passage.

0587-8   Hardcover
4663-5   Paperback